D1712680

Culture and Society in Shakespeare's Day

Backgrounds to Shakespeare
Culture and Society in Shakespeare's Day
Literature and the Theater in Shakespeare's Day
Shakespeare's Life

Culture and Society in Shakespeare's Day

Robert C. Evans

Sarah Fredericks and Deborah Cosier Solomon
Editorial Assistants

CHELSEA HOUSE
An Infobase Learning Company

Backgrounds to Shakespeare: Culture and Society in Shakespeare's Day
Copyright © 2012 by Infobase Publishing

Chelsea House
An imprint of Infobase Publishing
132 West 31st Street
New York, NY 10001

Library of Congress Cataloging-in-Publication Data
Evans, Robert C.
   Culture and society in Shakespeare's day / Robert C. Evans.
     p. cm. — (Backgrounds to Shakespeare)
   Includes bibliographical references and index.
   ISBN 978-1-60413-523-7 (acid-free paper)
   1. Shakespeare, William, 1564–1616—Homes and haunts—England.
2. Literature and society—England—History—16th century. 3. Literature and society—England—History—17th century. 4. England—Social life and customs—16th century. 5. England—Social life and customs—17th century. I. Title.
   PR2910.E93 2012
   942.05'5—dc23   2011043208

Chelsea House books are available at special discounts when purchased in bulk quantities for businesses, associations, institutions, or sales promotions. Please call our Special Sales Department in New York at (212) 967-8800 or (800) 322-8755.

You can find Chelsea House on the World Wide Web at
http://www.chelseahouse.com

Series design and composition by Erika K. Arroyo
Cover designed by Alicia Post
Cover printed by Yurchak Printing, Landisville, Pa.
Book printed and bound by Yurchak Printing, Landisville, Pa.
Date printed: March 2012

Printed in the United States of America

This book is printed on acid-free paper.

CONTENTS

PREFACE

This book focuses on the roughly six decades of English history, from 1564 to 1616, when William Shakespeare lived. His life coincided with one of the most interesting periods in the history of the British Isles. It was a period that saw the flourishing reign of one of the greatest English monarchs, Queen Elizabeth I, as well as the beginning of the union of England and Scotland during the reign of King James I. It was also a period in which Britain began to establish itself as a major world power and as a significant center of cultural accomplishment, especially in the field of literature. Finally, this was also a time of enormous political and religious tension, just as it was an era of significant changes in social and economic matters. This would be a fascinating period even if William Shakespeare had not been alive then.

The book focuses on life as it was lived in three major centers of English existence during this era: the countryside, London, and the royal court. I have tried, insofar as possible, to let contemporary witnesses speak at length and for themselves, so that their own distinctive voices and accents can be heard. Inevitably, I have had to draw on witnesses, such as William Harrison, whose testimony is often quoted by scholars, but I have also tried to call upon others — such as Thomas Tusser, George Herbert, and Leopold von Wedel — whose accounts are far less familiar. I hope that their reports and comments will help bring the period alive in ways that a more impersonal narrative might not. Whenever possible, I have tried through quotation to suggest some of the connections among topics discussed in this book and the treatment of such topics in Shakespeare's plays and poems. Unless otherwise noted, all quotations from Shakespeare are from the second *Riverside* edition. All quotations have been modernized in spelling.

DAILY LIFE IN THE COUNTRY

William Shakespeare lived in a society in which about 90 percent of the population dwelled in the countryside and earned its living through some sort of agricultural work—either by farming or by raising livestock, particularly sheep. People on the coasts or near rivers often fished for a living, and in some places mining coal was becoming a growing industry. In any case, the vast majority of people in Renaissance England lived close to the land or sea. They were in touch with the practical rhythms of rural life. The workday began with the rising of the sun, and most people were asleep by the time the sun set. Planting and harvesting crops and tending to livestock were the crucial events in the yearly cycle. A bad harvest or the spread of disease among animals could easily mean financial devastation or even starvation. Little wonder, then, that the blessings the goddess Ceres wishes on the young couple at the end of Shakespeare's *Tempest* include "Earth's increase, foison [abundance] plenty / Barns and garners never empty, / Vines and clustering bunches growing, / Plants with goodly burthen bowing." Little wonder, too, that Ceres concludes by proclaiming, "Spring come to you at the farthest / In the very end of harvest!" (4.1.11015). Everyone in Shakespeare's era knew the importance of agricultural success; their lives depended on it, and few people took it for granted, as many do today.

Indeed, England during this period was primarily an agricultural society. London, with a population in 1600 of approximately 200,000 people, was the only really large city in the country, although London was constantly growing, partly because some people were leaving the countryside. Fewer than 20 other towns had more than 5,000 inhabitants. In the rest of England, life revolved around small, often tiny rural villages surrounded by fields of crops, fields of sheep, and a diminishing number of forests. Larger market towns provided venues where rural folk could buy and sell their goods. Mills for grinding grain were a frequent feature of rural life, and some sense of the details of existence in the country can be glimpsed when Edgar, in *King Lear*, mentions beggars desperately seeking charity in the midst of "low farms, / poor pelting [paltry] villages, sheepcotes [sheep pens], and mills" (2.3.17–18).

Tourist map of Stratford-upon-Avon made by J. Ross Brown in about 1908.

FROM CROPS TO SHEEP

Most rural folk were relatively poor "tenant" farmers. They worked land not legally theirs. Instead the land was usually owned by wealthy local lords living on extensive manors in large manor houses. To these landowners, rent of various kinds—often crops or livestock—had to be paid. Increasingly, however, other wealthy people (often merchants) from towns or cities, especially London, were buying rural land, which was seen as a good investment. Many of these new owners were often distant, both literally and figuratively, from the people who actually worked the soil. For this reason and others, many of the open fields that had once been used for farming were being enclosed by fences, walls, or hedges. Thus, land that had once been used for raising crops could instead be used, more profitably, for raising sheep. People who had once earned their living by farming were increasingly unemployed, and often these people migrated to London to search for work.

The process of enclosing lands that had once seemed open or common caused a good deal of local resentment and sometimes resulted in strife and even riots. In such rioting, enclosures were sometimes violently—but only temporarily—torn down. The enclosure process seemed relentless. It was part of a larger, general movement in Shakespeare's England away from one kind of farming (farming that had once appeared communal) to a new kind that increasingly emphasized private property. In a complaint typical of the time, the unfortunately named Thomas Bastard wrote that "Sheep have eat up our meadows and our downs, / Our corn, our wood, whole villages and towns."

ATTRACTIONS OF THE COUNTRYSIDE

Despite the various real and undeniable problems of living in the countryside, life there also had its attractions. Fynes Moryson, in a book published in 1617 (the year after Shakespeare died), described the climate of England as temperate, with frequent rains, infrequent frosts, and snows that rarely lasted. He emphasized the many fruits that flourished in such a climate, including apricots, muskmelons, and figs. Moryson also reported that because of this generally pleasant climate, "all beasts bring forth their young in the open fields, even in the time of winter." He praised the abundance of "apples, pears, cherries and plums, such variety of them and so good in all respects, as no country yields more or better." But he also noted that the English forests in his day were "rather frequent and pleasant than vast, being exhausted for fire, and with iron-mills, so as the quantity of wood and charcoal for fire is much diminished." The growing population of the nation and even the growth of industry had begun to transform the English countryside. Nevertheless, Moryson also noted that wealth, even in rural areas, had its privileges: "[T]here is no country wherein the gentlemen and lords have so many large parks only reserved for the pleasure of hunting." He likewise reported that "all sorts of men allot . . . much ground about their houses for pleasure of gardens and orchards." Thus the Gardener in Shakespeare's *Richard II* instructs his assistant, "Go bind thou up yon dangling apricots, / Which, like unruly children, make their sire / Stoop with oppression of their prodigal weight" (3.4.29–31).

LIVESTOCK AND FOWL

Moryson's depiction of the English countryside as a green and pleasant land finds support in William Harrison's *Description of England*, first published in 1577 and then reprinted a decade later. Since Harrison wrote when Shakespeare was alive and still a youth, and since his *Description* is so extremely detailed, his book is exceptionally valuable. Harrison is quick to point out the various faults and shortcomings in the England of his day. Therefore, when he does offer praise, it seems generally trustworthy and can be supported from other sources, including modern scholarship.

Harrison depicts, for instance, a nation in which "horses, oxen, sheep, goats, [and] swine" abound, "far surmounting the like in other countries." He praises the quality and abundance of English milk and cheeses and the size of English horses, although he notes that asses and mules are rare. He considers English sheep "excellent" and says that for "sweetness of flesh they pass all other," but he notes that they are "often troubled by rot (as are our swine with the measles, though never so generally)." Harrison reports that in the English countryside, hogs were "kept by herds and an hogherd appointed to attend and wait upon them, who commonly gathereth them together by his noise and cry and leadeth them forth to feed in the fields." (One is reminded of Orlando's question in *As You Like It*: "Shall I keep your hogs, and eat husks with them?" [1.1.37–38].) Oddly enough, Harrison also notes that in some places women scoured and wet their clothes with the dung of hogs—a practice he found unappealing.

England was full of fowl both tame and wild, and Harrison lists and discusses most of them, including what he considered an overabundance of pigeons. Fowl were raised "in every farmer's yard" and were either "sold for ready money in the open markets" or consumed at home, often in great quantities. Harrison claims that when the English ate, "the whole carcasses of many capons, hens, pigeons, and suchlike do often go to wrack, beside beef, mutton, veal, and lamb, all which at every feast are taken for necessary dishes amongst the commonality of England." Obviously, the rich ate better than the poor, but various commentators of the time, including foreign observers, suggest that the English as a nation were unusually well fed. There was a strong emphasis on meat in their diets, including the meat of various fowl. Of course, annoying birds, especially ravens and crows, also abounded, and Parliament even endorsed unsuccessful efforts to exterminate them, as they were considered unclean and also "hurtful to poultry, conies [rabbits], lambs, and kids." On the other hand, some birds were prized for their songs, and Harrison notes that aviaries were increasingly established "for the better hearing of their melody and observation of their natures." Shakespeare's works are full of many pleasant references to birds, as when Bottom in *A Midsummer Night's Dream* mentions "The finch, the sparrow, and the lark, / The plainsong cuckoo grey, / Whose note full many a man doth mark" (3.1.130–33). Birds and animals of all sorts would have been a greater part of the daily experience of Shakespeare and his contemporaries than they tend to be for most people today.

CROPS, FRUITS, AND FLOWERS

Of the crops grown in Shakespeare's England, *corn* was the general name for most kinds of edible grains, including what we now call wheat. "Corn" in the modern American sense (as in "corn on the cob") had not begun to be imported from the New World. One gets a sense of the variety of crops that might count as "corn" when Harrison remarks that

> The bread throughout the land is made of such grain as the soil yieldeth; nevertheless, the gentility [wealthier people] commonly provide themselves sufficiently of wheat for their own tables, whilst their household [that is, servants] and poor neighbors in some shires are enforced to content themselves with rye or barley, yea, and in time of dearth, many with bread made either of beans, peason [peas], or oats, or of all together and some acorns among, of which scourge the poorest do soonest taste, since they are least able to provide themselves of better.

Ceres (the goddess from whose name the word *cereal* is derived) is associated in Shakespeare's *Tempest* with "wheat, rye, barley, vetches [beans], oats and pease" (4.1.61), and all of those crops would have been readily familiar to Shakespeare and his contemporaries.

Planting, tending, and harvesting such crops were the main tasks of most of the population of rural England, including husbands, wives, and even small children. Other crops, too, were also raised, including, Harrison writes, "melons, pompions [pumpkins], gourds, cucumbers, radishes, skirrets [a kind of parsnip], parsnips, carrots, cabbages, navews [coles], turnips, and all kinds of salad herbs." These were eaten by rich and poor alike. Flowers were raised in gardens not only for beauty but as potential sources of medicine, and various kinds of plants previously unknown in England were being imported from abroad: "[M]any strange herbs, plants, and annual fruits," Harrison notes, "are daily brought unto us from the Indies, Americans, Taprobane [Ceylon], Canary Isles, and all parts of the world." Other edibles raised in the countryside included "apples, plums, pears, walnuts, filberts, . . . apricots, almonds, peaches, [and] figs." Moreover, grafting had begun to produce "artificial mixtures, whereby one tree bringeth forth sundry fruits and one and the same fruit of diverse colors and tastes." Shakespeare alludes to this process in Act 3, scene 2 of *As You Like It*, and there is abundant evidence that he, like most residents of England, was highly familiar with many details of agricultural life in the English countryside.

BIRTH, MARRIAGE, AND DEATH

For people living in Shakespeare's England, according to Jeffrey L. Singman, three of the major events of life—birth, marriage, and death—revolved, as most things did, around the church. Babies were usually born at home with midwives or other women in attendance, but baptism was supposed to take place fairly quickly in the local parish church. There the birth of the child would be recorded and he or she would become part of the eternal Christian community and receive a "Christian name." Godparents participated in the ceremony, and later the mother of the child would go to church again for a ceremony known as "churching," which was intended to give thanks for the successful birth.

Elizabethans tended to divide life into periods of seven years each. At age seven a child was thought to have reached the age of reason and was now responsible for his or her actions. At age 14, puberty conventionally began; 21 was the conventional age of adulthood. It was not until most young men and women reached this latter age that marriage usually took place, and many men waited until they were closer to 30 before marrying, because it was cru-

Photograph of Shakespeare's birthplace Stratford-upon-Avon, published by Poulton in the nineteenth century.

THE YEARLY RURAL ROUTINE

Many of the details of rural existence are outlined, month by month, in a work by Nicholas Breton titled *Fantastickes* and published in 1626, 10 years after Shakespeare's death. Although Breton's prose is often somewhat

cial that the couple be financially independent. A couple's intention to marry was usually announced three times in the local church before being finally solemnized there. Just as births were recorded in the church's register, so were marriages, and the rules of the church meant that most marriages lasted until the death of one of the parties. Divorce was highly unusual.

Death also involved the church. Bells rang in the parish church immediately after a person's death, and corpses were buried either inside the church (if the person had been prominent) or outside in the parish churchyard. Deaths, like births and marriages, were recorded in the parish register.

"... thou met'st with things dying,
I with things new-born."
— *The Winter's Tale* (3.3.113–14)

William Shakespeare's grave in the Holy Trinity Church, Stratford-upon-Avon, England. This photograph was taken in June of 2007. (*Photograph by David Jones; used under a Creative Commons license*)

whimsical, he gives a vivid sense of what it was like to be alive in rural England during a typical year. He notes, for instance, that in January, "The load horse to the mill hath his full back burden, and the thresher in the barn tries the strength of his flail." In February, Breton reports, "The hunting horse is at the heels of the hound," while "The trees a little begin to bud, and the sap begins to rise up out of the root." In March, "The football now trieth the legs of strength, and merry matches [of rural sports] continue good fellowship." April arrives, and

> the nightingale begins to tune her throat against May. The sunny showers perfume the air, and the bees begin to go abroad for honey; the dew, as in pearls, hangs upon the tops of the grass, while the turtles [doves] sit billing upon the little green boughs; the trout begins to play in the brooks, and the salmon leaves the sea to play in the fresh waters.

With the coming of May, "the fowler [bird catcher] makes ready his whistle for the quail; the lark sets the morning watch, and the evening the nightingale," while "The chicken and the duck are fattened for the market, and many a gosling never lives to be a goose." By June, Breton notes, hay has already grown tall enough for reaping, and "the haymakers are mustered to make an army for the field," with implements for both male and female reapers. "The trees are all in their rich array," but each individual sheep, in contrast, "is turned out of his coat."

In July, according to Breton, "The stag and the buck are now in pride of their time, and the hardness of their heads makes them fit for the horn" of hunting, while in August, "Now begin the gleaners to follow the corn cart, and a little bread to a great deal of drink makes the travailer's [worker's] dinner. The melon and the cucumber is now in request, and oil and vinegar give attendance on the sallet [salad] herbs." By September, "the meadows are left bare by the mouths of hungry cattle, and the hogs are turned into the cornfields. The winds begin to knock the apples' heads together on the trees, and the fallings are gathered to fill the pies for the householder." In October, Breton notes, "the hogs in the woods grow fat with the fallen acorns; the forward deer begin to go to rut, and the barren doe groweth good meat. The basket-makers now gather their rods, and the fishers lay their leaps [traps] in the deep; the load horses go apace to the mill, and the meat-market is seldom without people." Yet by November, Breton somberly reports, "The winds are now cold and the air chill, and the poor die through want of charity."

Finally, in December, "capons and hens, besides turkeys, geese and ducks, besides beef and mutton, must all die for the great [Christmas] feast, for in twelve days a multitude of people will not be fed with a little." Christmas was for many the highlight of the year, for, as Marcellus remarks in *Hamlet*, "so hallowed and so gracious is that time" (1.1.164).

Not everyone, of course, ate as well as Breton suggests, as his comment about the dying poor clearly implies. Nevertheless, the sentences quoted, as well as Breton's entire description of the 12 months, suggest just how much the English year, especially in rural areas, revolved around raising, gathering, and consuming food. Almost all people—even, or perhaps especially, the very poor—had to focus on the food supply. Today, in modern advanced societies, we tend to assume that that supply will always and simply be there, but people in Shakespeare's era could never afford to be so complacent. The Egyptian farmers described in *Antony and Cleopatra* could tell from the rise and fall of the Nile "if dearth / Or foison [abundant harvests]" would follow (2.7.1394–95), and the residents of Shakespeare's England would have been just as attuned to such matters in their own day.

FISHING AND OTHER INDUSTRIES

The rhythms of the rural year were set by the rhythms of food production, and this was just as true on the coasts as in the interior. Harrison, for instance, notes that "As our fowls, therefore, have their seasons, so likewise have all our sorts of sea fish, whereby it cometh to pass that none, or at leastwise very few of them, are to be had at all times." He then lists the various kinds of fish that were most plentifully found in any given month. Although he claims to be far from an expert in such matters, he clearly appreciates the contributions that English fishers made to the vitality of the country's economy and to the diversity of its diet. One thinks of the comment made by Pericles in one of Shakespeare's late plays: "Peace be at your labour, honest fishermen" (*Pericles*, 2.1.52). Partly to encourage the prosperity of the English fishing industry and to promote the size of the English fleet, the government decreed that only fish—not other kinds of meat—could be eaten on certain days of the week and at certain times of the year.

Fishing, however, was not the only way, besides raising crops and livestock, that people in rural England supported themselves. Coal mining has already been mentioned, and Harrison also refers to the "pits or mines, out of which we dig our stone to build withal." Most homes, though (at least those owned by people with decent incomes), were still built with timber or, increasingly, with bricks, and so brick making was another form of livelihood. Nevertheless, Harrison considered it wasteful to use artificial brick rather than the plentiful stone with which "Almighty God" had "so blessed our realm." He reports that because fire was used to prepare the brick, "a great part of the wood of this land is daily consumed and spent, to the no small decay of that commodity and hindrance of the poor, that perish oft for cold."

The high price of fuel was a source of constant concern, as was a chronic shortage of housing. The rural poor typically had to endure very primitive living conditions, often crammed into mere one-room huts along with any animals they might own. Such people found work whenever and however they could. Most of them, ironically, worked in the fields, mines, stone pits, and brick factories that helped support the rest of the growing economy while providing little income to the workers themselves. Sheep raising and sheep shearing, for instance, provided employment for many people living in the countryside, and wool was England's most important export. Harrison, however, passionately regretted that English wool was "dressed abroad, while our clothworkers here do starve and beg their bread and for lack of daily practice utterly neglect to be skillful in this science!"

THE RURAL POOR

Many of the people in rural and coastal England were poor folk. Shakespeare's awareness of their plight helped inspire King Lear's memorable lines when he suddenly finds himself practically alone and homeless in a violent storm:

> Poor naked wretches, whereso'er you are,
> That bide the pelting of this pitiless storm,
> How shall your homeless heads and unfed sides,
> Your loop'd and windowed raggedness, defend you
> From seasons such as these?
>
> (*King Lear*, 3.4.28–32)

Finding and keeping proper shelter were not hypothetical problems in a drama for the stage. Rather, they were the kind of hard, practical concerns faced by many an Englishman and Englishwoman, especially anyone living in the countryside, where poverty was common.

The ever-helpful Harrison divided the poor of England into three basic categories. First there were the poor "by impotency, as the fatherless child, the aged blind, and the diseased person that is judged to be incurable." Second were those who were "poor by casualty, as the wounded soldier, the decayed householder, and the sick person visited with grievous and painful diseases." Finally there were the "thriftless poor," such as the improvident

> rioter that hath consumed all, the vagabond that will abide nowhere but runneth up and down from place to place (as it were seeking work and finding none), and finally the rogue and strumpet, which are not possible to be divided in sunder but run to and fro over all the realm, chiefly keeping the champaign soils [that is, open fields used for farming] in summer to avoid the scorching heat, and the woodland grounds in winter to eschew the blustering winds.

Most people in England felt that the first two kinds of poor people deserved public assistance, and taxes were levied in each parish to help support them. English Protestants were proud that their country provided as well as it did for the deserving poor, especially because Catholics at home and abroad often alleged that Henry VIII's break with the old Roman Catholic faith had also meant a breakdown in Christian charity for the needy.

Even when they required no public assistance, however, most people living in England, especially those living in the countryside, were by no means wealthy, and even the wealthiest lived harder lives than we are accustomed to today. Everyone of every status, for instance, was far more affected by the climate—the cold of the winter, the heat of the summer, and frequent dampness year-round—than tends to be true in modern times. Sickness was common and often fatal; effective medicines were rare; fleas and lice abounded; and sanitation was primitive by modern standards. It is easy to romanticize English rural existence in Shakespeare's era, partly because Shakespeare himself romanticized it to some degree in such wonderful plays as *As You Like It*, but the darker aspects of life in the English countryside of his period should never be forgotten. Life was especially grim for the rural poor, as plays such as *King Lear* definitely remind us.

RURAL ARISTOCRATS

For the tiny segment of the population at the top of the rural hierarchy— the aristocrats, the gentry, and the rich in their often lavish estates and manors—life in the countryside had real attractions. Thus the famous poem "To Penshurst," written by Shakespeare's friendly competitor, the poet and dramatist Ben Jonson, extols the beautiful rural estate of the powerful Sidney family. Jonson contrasts Penshurst with the lavish "prodigy houses"

RELIGIOUS CONFLICT IN SHAKESPEARE'S ENGLAND

Roman Catholicism had been the traditional religion of England—and indeed of most of western Europe—for many hundreds of years before Shakespeare's time. By the sixteenth century, however, efforts to reform the religion ("the Reformation") had actually led "Protestants" to break from the old faith. Partly this break was due to the perceived corruption of the Roman Church; more fundamentally it was rooted in serious doctrinal differences between Protestants and traditional Catholics. In England, the break from Rome had initially been caused more by political conflict than by doctrinal disagreement: King Henry VIII wished to divorce his first wife, who had failed to produce the male heir Henry desired, but the pope had refused to allow the divorce. Henry therefore broke with Rome, abolished the authority of the pope in England, abolished Catholic monasteries and other institutions, and set himself up as head of a separate English (or "Anglican") church.

Many people in England were far more serious and committed Protestants than Henry was, including his own son, who became King Edward VI when Henry died. Edward was surrounded by Protestant advisers who hoped the young king would advance the cause of the Protestant Reformation in England, but Edward died before the process could be completed. He was succeeded by his half sister Mary, a devout Catholic whose husband was Philip II, Spain's Catholic king. Mary and Philip tried to return England to the Catholic fold, often by violent means, but Mary died before the old faith could be firmly reestablished. She was followed on the throne by her half sister, Elizabeth, who was a sincere Protestant but tried to achieve a kind of middle way (via media) in governing the church. Neither extreme Catholics nor extreme Protestants (often called "Puritans") were pleased by the queen's moderation, but her stance seems to have satisfied most of the population.

> In religion,
> What damnèd error but some sober brow
> Will bless it, and approve it with a text . . .
> — *The Merchant of Venice* (3.2.77–80)

that were being built in the countryside by so many other wealthy people during Shakespeare's era. These latter homes—such as Hatfield House, built by the supremely influential Sir Robert Cecil—were massive and splendid and often boasted the latest in architectural innovations. Ironically, though, the cost of building them sometimes bankrupted the people whose wealth

Portrait of Princess Elizabeth I, ca. 1546. *(Attributed to William Scrots)*

they were meant to display. Contrasting Penshurst with such homes, Jonson celebrates the Sidney estate as a place that "joy'st in better marks of soil, of air, / Of wood, of water; therein thou art fair" (7–8). He describes the magnificent trees and forests of Penshurst, its abundance of deer, its numerous sheep and cattle and horses, its plentiful rabbits and wildfowl, and its ponds brimming with fish. Penhurst's orchards were full of fruit and its gardens full of flowers, and Jonson reports how

The early cherry, with the later plum,
    Fig, grape, and quince, each in his time doth come.
The blushing apricot and wooly peach
    Hang on thy walls that every child may reach. (41–44)

Inside the massive home itself, the Sidneys and their many guests were well supplied with meat and bread and beer and wine, and the servants who watched as the Sidneys and their guests consumed such food were themselves well fed afterward, according to Jonson.

"To Penshurst" may well have been the first of the new genre of "country house poems"—a kind of poetry that became immediately popular, partly because it celebrated an ideal of virtuous country living that many English people of Jonson's and Shakespeare's day held dear. Jonson wrote another important country house poem, "To Sir Robert Wroth," that echoes many of the details of "To Penshurst." Once again Jonson mentions abundant livestock, beautiful meadows, and the hunting of deer, wildfowl, and rabbits, and he also celebrates the growth of grain, the harvesting of apples, and the

Penshurst Place, the rural estate of the Sidney family. Ben Jonson extols the virtues of the estate in his poem "To Penshurst."

abundance of food and drink. And, as also in "To Penshurst," he mentions the intermixture of social classes—the ways that local magnates, such as the Wroths and Sidneys, could sometimes be hospitable to the far less wealthy people who lived on or around their estates, in the countryside and nearby villages. This ideal of hospitality was obviously not practiced nearly as often as Jonson and many others would have wished, but it clearly was an ideal that his poems and other such writings were meant to extol and propagate.

THE RURAL GENTRY

The aristocrats and the enormously wealthy were not the only people who had good reason to enjoy living in the country. The Earl of Shaftesbury, for instance, describes the life of Henry Hastings, a country gentleman who was born in 1551 and who died nearly a century later in 1650. Shaftesbury notes that Hastings's "house was perfectly of the old fashion, in the midst of a large park well stocked with deer, and near the house rabbits to serve his kitchen, many fish-ponds, and great store of wood and timber." Hastings owned a private bowling green, and he "kept all manner of sport hounds that ran buck, fox, hare, otter and badger, and hawks long and short winged; he had all sorts of nets for fishing." Inside his home, "The parlour was a large, long room

Illustration of Longleat House, an Elizabethan country manor house. *(Illustration by Henry Thew Stephenson)*

. . . properly furnished; on a great hearth paved with brick lay some terriers and the choicest hounds and spaniels." Shaftesbury describes at length Hastings's devotion to hunting, but he also notes that one room in Hastings's house "had two small tables and a desk, on the one side of which was a church Bible, on the other the Book of Martyrs"—details that remind us of the central importance of the Christian religion in the lives of most people in Shakespeare's England.

Near these religious works in Hastings's home, however, were also backgammon "tables, dice, [and] cards," and in "the hole of the desk were store of tobacco-pipes." Tobacco was, for many English people, one of the great personal benefits of the discovery of the New World, although Shakespeare never mentions the drug in a single of his works. Many people had become strongly addicted to it, much to the chagrin of various moralists. Yet however much Hastings may have been attracted to tobacco, he was at least, according to Shaftesbury, a moderate drinker, even though his house was well supplied with "strong beer and wine."

Various kinds of food were also plentiful in Hastings's home, such as "a cold chine of beef, pasty of venison, gammon of bacon, or great apple-pie, with the thick crust extremely baked." Hastings's own hunting provided all the meats he needed aside from "beef and mutton, except Friday, when he had the best sea-fish as well as other fish he could get." To wash down such foods, he "drank a glass of wine or two at meals" and "always a tun glass without feet stood by him holding a pint of small beer, which he often stirred with a great sprig of rosemary." Shaftesbury reports that Hastings "was well-natured, but soon angry, calling his servants bastards and cuckoldy knaves"—a detail reminding us that his estate, like all estates, was a small social hierarchy—a kind of kingdom of its own—in which the lord of the manor definitely occupied the top position. Shaftesbury notes that Hastings "lived to a hundred, never lost his eyesight, but always writ and read without spectacles, and got to horse without help. Until past fourscore [years] he rode to the death of a stag as well as any." "Hunting," as one of Shakespeare's characters says of another person, "was his daily exercise" (*Henry VI*, Part III [4.6.85]), and perhaps such exercise even contributed to Hastings's long life.

THE RURAL YEOMEN FARMERS

Just as gentry such as Hastings were lower in the social scale than aristocrats such as the Sidneys or Wroths, so there was an even larger class of people below the gentry—a grouping known as "yeomen." "This sort of people," Harrison remarked,

> have a certain pre-eminence and more estimation than laborers and the common sort of artificers, and these commonly live wealthily, keep good houses, and travail [work] to get riches. They are also for the most part farmers to gentlemen . . . or at the leastwise artificers; and with grazing, frequenting of markets, and keeping of servants (not idle servants as the gentlemen do, but such as get both their own and part of their master's living) do come to great wealth, insomuch that many of them are able and do buy the lands of unthrifty gentlemen. . . .

In this last remark, one catches a glimpse of the kind of social mobility, both upward and downward, that was increasingly common during Shakespeare's era. Shakespeare's own father both rose and fell financially, and Shakespeare himself would eventually rise impressively, both in status and in wealth. Similar kinds of changes were taking place in the lives of many citizens of England during Shakespeare's era, not only in the cities but also in the countryside.

What was life like for an English rural yeoman and his family? As Harrison's description implies, many yeomen in the country were relatively prosperous farmers, residing in reasonably comfortable homes (often in or near villages), employing both male and female servants, and able to live, for the most part, off the products of their own farms. Many yeomen would have been interested in rising, or in seeing their sons rise, into the ranks of the gentry or gentlefolk (a group defined as people who did not have to work with their hands for a living). The intense social ambition of yeomen was proverbial, and it is even alluded to in Shakespeare's *King Lear,* when the fool remarks that "he's a mad yeoman that sees his son a gentleman before him" (3.6.13–14).

Yet many yeomen would also have worried that they, after a series of bad harvests or the spread of disease among their livestock, might fall into the ranks of the unfortunate peasantry or country laborers. To help prevent any such decline, yeomen spent much of their time working their land and also supervising the labor of others. A yeoman farmer would have been intimately familiar with the diseases of his animals and greatly concerned with good weather for his crops. Many yeomen were on a constant lookout to acquire new land and expand their farms, and many supplemented the income they made from farming crops by also raising sheep and selling wool.

Many of the details of the typical life of yeoman farmers can be glimpsed by reading *A Hundreth Good Pointes of Husbandrie* by Thomas Tusser (1524–1580), who was a farmer. This book was first printed in 1557, but it proved so successful that Tusser soon enlarged it to include 500 points altogether, all delivered in unpretentious rhymed couplets. Tusser begins, for instance, by emphasizing the importance of concord between a farmer and his wife, as a wife was the farmer's most important partner in work as in other ways. Frequently servants were supervised not only by the farmer but also by his wife (especially if the servants were women), and indeed wives played key roles in helping any farm prosper. Besides spinning wool and preparing meals, wives, according to Tusser, had a special obligation to be thrifty and help their husbands save for the future. He considered a solid, cooperative marriage crucial to the success of any yeoman's farm.

Besides offering much other counsel, Tusser advised farmers to be dedicated, thrifty, and not too lavish in their Sunday meals, and he also emphasized the importance of rewarding good work and good workers:

> Good labouring threshers, are worthy to eat:
> Good husbandly ploughmen, deserveth their meat.
> Good huswively huswives, that let for no rest
> should eat when they list [want to], and should drink of the best.

On the other hand, Tusser warned, a successful yeoman farmer needed to be wary of slothful workers, especially if they were also petty thieves. The farmer needed to supervise his workers well, making sure they did a thorough job of harvesting crops, and the farmer needed to know how to buy and sell prudently. Seeds had to be properly sown and carefully tended; different kinds of crops had to be planted during particular months; and crows had to be scared (often by boys) away from all kinds of tempting "corn." Rye needed to be harvested in September, and wheat had to be reaped by the end of October. New livestock sometimes needed to be purchased and fattened; mast (forest nuts) had to be set aside to feed swine during times of frost; and hogs had to be protected from the marauding hounds of neighbors. Wood had to be collected and stowed for burning, especially before winter arrived, and Tusser advised that the provident farmer should "Get ever before hand, drag never behind: / lest winter beclip [seize] thee, and break off thy mind."

Grain, Tusser advised, needed to be carefully stored in the barn; any work in the barn needed to be supervised by the farmer himself; and some of the grain needed to be set aside to feed the farm's workhorses. Plough horses were particularly valuable and deserved special care. Cattle needed to be kept warm and dry and carefully—and even variously—fed:

> Serve first out thy rye straw, then wheat & then peas:
> then oatstraw then barley, then hay if thou please.
> But serve them with hay, while thy straw stoover [winter food] last:
> they love no more straw, they had rather to fast.

Butchering of livestock, according to Tusser, should begin around the end of October and continue each week until early February, and beef and bacon in particular should be set aside for the Easter feast. Even before then, however, Christmas should be properly celebrated:

> At Christmas be merry, and thank God of all:
> and feast thy poor neighbours, the great with the small.
> yea all the year long, have an eye to the poor,
> and God shall send luck, to keep open thy door.

Nevertheless, Tusser advised that when the Christmas season had ended, the farmer should stop feasting and get back to his normal routine of arduous work, including the maintaining of livestock. He thought calves born between New Year's and Lent were more likely to survive the next winter, having already experienced some cold, whereas calves born later, in the spring, might just as well be killed because they would probably not prove hardy. Six was the ideal number of piglets for each sow, in Tusser's view; any more than that were unlikely to survive. Horses should be gelded or not gelded depending on their eventual use: Horses meant to be ridden should be gelded, while horses intended to pull carts should not be. Likewise, only the strongest-looking mares should be used for breeding. A good milk cow was profitable, but a good sow was even more so. Cattle should be well fed and well watered so they would grow and thrive. Meanwhile, planting an orchard was a splendid idea: Orchards provided both plenty and profit, and any such combination was always welcome. Even Shallow, in Shakespeare's *2 Henry IV,* is able to promise, "Nay, you shall see my orchard, where, in an arbor, / we will eat a last year's pippin [apple] of mine own graffing [grafting]" (5.3.1–3).

In employing servants, Tusser thought, a yeoman farmer needed to beware of hiring varlets or prostitutes, but good servants should be highly valued and treated well. Good servants, for instance, should receive their fair share of homemade cheese, lest they seek employment elsewhere. Servants, in return, had various duties, including assisting with practically every one of the farmer's own jobs. Besides caring for livestock, weeding crops, shearing sheep, and helping with harvests and household tasks, they were often set to work making harvest tools and repairing farm equipment, such as leaking carts. When harvesttime returned, Tusser opined, the farmer was like the captain of an army of servant-soldiers. He had to work alongside them in the hot sun, but when the harvest was successfully finished, he should play the genial host and "welcome [his] harvest folk, servants and all: / with mirth and good cheer."

> Thy harvest thus ended, in mirth and in joy:
> please every one gently, man woman and boy.
> Thus doing, with alway, such help as they can:
> thou winnest the name, of a right husbandman.

As Tusser's book and many other sources make clear, the lives of a yeoman farmer, his wife, his children, and his servants involved constant work of a wide variety. Such people rose early and were usually in bed by dark, and their waking hours were mainly hours of labor.

RURAL TOWNS AND VILLAGES

In terms of work, the lives of yeomen and their families would not have differed much from the lives of most other "common" people living in rural England, especially the small businessmen and nonagricultural workers who dwelled in English villages and small towns. Such latter folk would have included bakers, bricklayers, carpenters, cloth workers, coopers, glassmakers, innkeepers, masons, mercers, merchants, metalworkers, millers, miners, shopkeepers, tailors, tinkers, vintners, weavers, and even glove makers (the trade of Shakespeare's father). The English common folk in the countryside, villages, and towns of Shakespeare's day were industrious and hardworking people. They had to be; they might not survive otherwise.

The towns and villages in which many people lived were small—often tiny—and were surrounded by fields and pastures. Neighbors were well known to one another; the kind of anonymous privacy that is increasingly a feature of modern urban life was unknown then. Families were central to the social structure of life in villages and small towns and on farms and manors, and families generally were headed by fathers, who enjoyed much more authority than tends to be true today. Wives were often well loved by their mates and highly valued as partners in every aspect of existence (including business), but they were clearly subordinate to their men. Likewise, children were subordinate to their parents; there was little of the catering to children that is often typical today. When children were not in school (and not every child by any means was offered an education), they were helping with the work involved in running the family enterprise. In the towns and villages as on the farms, simple survival was the first task of each family.

RURAL RELIGION

Religion played an important role in the lives of most who lived in the countryside and in the lives of most residents of villages and towns. Most villages had a parish church, and church attendance—especially on Sundays—was expected. The church was one of the crucial hubs of village life; it was where most residents of a rural community would come together at least once a week. It was the place where marriages occurred, where babies were christened, and where funerals took place. Surrounding each village church was often a churchyard full of the graves of those who had lived in the village. Inside the church, wealthier families often commissioned sculptures and carvings to commemorate their own dead. Indeed, the church was one of the places in the village where members of various social classes met and mixed. During the era of religious turmoil that followed Henry VIII's break with the Roman Catholic Church, religion was an even more important issue for most English people than it had been in the past.

The idea of religious pluralism—of allowing each person to choose his or her own faith—is something we often take for granted today, but in Shakespeare's time almost everyone supported the idea of an official state religion. They simply disagreed, often violently, about which religion that should be. Catholics wanted to revive the "old faith"; Protestants wanted to protect and expand the new dispensation; and some Protestants (known as Puritans) wanted to transform the English church in even more radical ways. Many of the people living in Shakespeare's England had once been Catholics or at least had parents or grandparents who had been. Open Catholic worship now was forbidden, however; the nation was officially Protestant, specifically Anglican. The churches in England's villages and towns belonged to the Church of England, and the people of England were expected to belong

Portrait of Henry VIII, 1540. *(Hans Holbein)*

to that church as well. The abolition of the Roman Catholic faith and the expropriation of its buildings and land had meant a financial windfall for many wealthy (and even not-so-wealthy) people living in the countryside, but many people, at least at first, must have missed the old faith, the old rituals, and the old rhythms of the Catholic year. Some Catholics, known as "recusants," refused to take communion in the Protestant churches, but even they were expected to attend services.

In villages and towns across England, the interiors of churches were transformed in efforts to remove all vestiges of Catholic "idolatry." Depictions of the saints and the Virgin Mary and other sorts of Catholic lore were painted over or stripped from the walls; the number of sacraments was radically reduced; and sermons were now in English, rather than in Latin. Harrison notes that in his time

> all images, shrines, tabernacles, rood lofts, and monuments of idolatry
> are removed, taken down, and defaced; only the stories in glass
> windows excepted, for want of sufficient store of new stuff and by
> reason of extreme charge [expense] that should grow by the alteration
> of the same into white panes throughout the realm, are not altogether
> abolished in most places at once but by little and little suffered to
> decay, that white glass may be provided and set up in their rooms.

Many a Protestant in Shakespeare's day would have agreed with words from a different context in *Troilus and Cressida*: "'Tis mad idolatry / To make the service greater than the god" (2.2.56–57).

Knowledge of the Bible was cultivated through constant public readings of the scriptures in the native tongue. Harrison noted that "the Psalter is said over once in thirty days, the New Testament four times, and the Old Testament once in the year." Unfortunately, not all preachers were well educated, nor were there enough preachers—qualified or unqualified—for every single church. Therefore "certain sermons or homilies" were preprepared by the government and the church hierarchy for public delivery, as these could be read aloud even by priests without much learning of their own.

A partial list of the topics emphasized in these authorized sermons and homilies gives a good sense of the flavor of religious instruction in Shakespeare's era. The sermons stressed such themes as the reading of Holy Scripture, the misery of all mankind, the salvation of all people, the traits of a true and lively faith, the proper role of good works, the importance of Christian love and charity, and the problem of fearing death. Other topics included the proper use of the church, the perils of idolatry, the need to keep churches repaired and clean, the benefits of fasting, the purposes of prayer, rules regarding sacraments, the importance of giving alms, and the ideals of marriage. The significance of various holy days—such as the Nativity, Good Friday, Easter, and Whitsunday—was explained, and one sermon particularly emphasized the need for repentance of sin and true reconciliation with God. Not all the teachings, however, were so heavily theological; some were also practical and had real implications for day-to-day social life. Sermons denounced swearing and lying, whoredom and adultery, and strife, contention, and idleness; there was even a sermon against disobedience and willful rebellion. The sermons and homilies were intended to produce not only good Christians but also peaceful, law-abiding, and compliant citizens. Duke Senior, living in the countryside in *As You Like It*, finds "Sermons in stones" (2.1.17), but there were plenty of real sermons to be heard in rural England.

RURAL PARISH PRIESTS

The parish priest was one of the most important citizens in any village or town. He not only preached the word of God but was also expected to lead an exemplary Christian life and thus provide a model for his parishioners. Harrison felt that the priests of the Anglican church were superior to their Roman Catholic predecessors in part because they could marry. Thus, "their meat and drink is more orderly and frugally dressed, their furniture of household more convenient and better looked unto, and the poor oftener fed generally than heretofore they have been." George Herbert, the great religious poet who was also a country priest, cautioned that an unmarried priest should never talk "with any woman alone, but in the audience of others, and that seldom, and then also in a serious manner, never jestingly or sportfully." According to Herbert, a country parson needed to be "very circumspect in all companies, both of his behaviour, speech, and very looks, knowing himself to be both suspected and envied." Everyone in a village or small town was subject to observation and potential censure, and this was perhaps especially true of the local minister. A married priest, Herbert thought, had to choose wisely the kind of wife who would be good and wise, and he should treat her with respect, especially in front of her servants.

Herbert's book, commonly known as *The Country Parson*, is especially valuable because, in outlining the responsibilities of a parish priest, it also provides many important details about parish life in general. The country parson, Herbert thought, should be "very exact in the governing of his house, making it a copy and model for his Parish." His wife, who should be godly, should help him raise godly children, and she should not only be skilled in curing sickness but should also be a competent partner in managing domestic affairs and keeping the family out of debt. The parson, Herbert thought, should raise his children as good Christians and good citizens, and he should begin to groom them, especially his sons, from an early age for their adult professions and responsibilities. Some of his children should be sent off to work as apprentices in the homes of skilled craftsmen or other small businessmen, and the parson, like any good father, should never "omit

South East Prospect of Stratford upon Avon. 1746.

A 1746 engraving of the southeast view of Stratford-upon-Avon. *(Illustration by R. Greene)*

any present good deed of charity in consideration of providing a stock for his children." Herbert felt that a parson should additionally make sure that his servants were also religious, since a household attended by religious servants "is blessed and prospers." Every member of a parson's household should seek to have a good influence on the rest of the village or town. The personal, religious, and civic virtues that Herbert seeks to instill in the family of his country parson would have been virtues prized by most of the respectable families in the countryside of Shakespeare's era.

Herbert suggests that the country parson, in dealing with his servants and children, should sometimes show love and sometimes instill fear. In running and furnishing his household, he should exercise modesty and moderation. He should care for the many poor, showing them hospitality as well as financial generosity. The parson should try to ensure that "there be not a beggar or idle person in his Parish, but that all be in a competent way of getting their living." The parson should seek to achieve this goal "either by bounty, or persuasion, or by authority, making use of that excellent statute which binds all Parishes to maintain their own." No poor person, however, should be allowed to rely on charity as if it were a kind of guaranteed pension or reliable inheritance. Rather, charity should be used to encourage people to be more religious and to work harder at providing for themselves. The parson, Herbert thought, should be generous to anyone who needed help, especially the sick, and he should also encourage such generosity in others.

In describing the ideal parish church, Herbert's sentences often resemble those of Harrison, who wrote several decades earlier. Herbert expects that the church should be kept "in good repair: as walls plastered, windows glazed, floor paved, [and] seats whole, firm, and uniform." The church should be "swept and kept clean, without dust or cobwebs, and at great festivals [it should be] strawed, and stuck with boughs, and perfumed with incense." In addition, Herbert continued,

> there should be fit and proper texts of Scripture every where painted, and
> . . . all the painting [should] be grave and reverend, not with light colors or foolish antics. [Furthermore], . . . all the books appointed by Authority [should] be there, and those not torn, or fouled, but whole; and clean, and well bound.

This, at least, was the ideal, and it was an ideal probably achieved in many of the small churches of Shakespeare's time. The Christian religion was crucial to the lives of most of the population, and church buildings themselves were perhaps the most important buildings in most villages and towns. Churches were the social centers of most villages, small towns, and rural communities and possessed a great deal of legal, moral, and spiritual authority.

LIVES OF RURAL PARISHIONERS

Herbert's book also offers valuable insights into the lives of the country parson's parishioners. At one point, for instance, Herbert advises parsons to visit their parishioners unexpectedly, during the workweek, when he can observe them as they really are. On Sundays, Herbert cautions, people can put on different habits of conduct in the same ways they put on clean clothes, only to be taken off again the next day. By visiting them during the workweek, however, the parson could see them in their everyday lives. With any luck, he would find some of them reading (in which case he should supply them with religious books) or caring for the sick (in which case he should supply them with helpful prescriptions). If he happened to find parishioners working at their jobs, he should commend them for doing so but also remind them how to work in the proper spirit. He should advise them not to

> labour anxiously, nor distrustfully, nor profanely. [For] they labour anxiously when they overdo it, to the loss of their quiet and health; then distrustfully, when they doubt God's providence, thinking that their own labour is the cause of their thriving, as if it were in their own hands to thrive or not to thrive. *Then they labour profanely, when they set themselves to work like brute beasts, never raising their thoughts to God, nor sanctifying their labour with daily prayer; when on the Lord's day they do unnecessary servile work, or in time of divine service on other holy days, except in the cases of extreme poverty, and in seasons of Seed-time or Harvest* [italics in original].

As these words suggest, a real problem for many of the people living in Shakespeare's era was the problem of working too much—of being so concerned with supporting themselves and their families that they felt they couldn't pause to rest or take time to honor God. Yet even Herbert, concerned as he was with the problem of excessive or obsessive labor, admitted that times of planting and harvesting were special cases and that extreme poverty necessitated extreme devotion to work. Herbert once again reminds the parson of his responsibility to aid those who are extremely poor—a reminder to him and to us that such poverty was not uncommon in Shakespeare's day. However, if the parson did find any people who were "idle, or ill-employed," he should, according to Herbert, remonstrate with them and suit his advice to his audience, being blunt with plain countrymen but more indirect with those capable of responding to hints. He should not hesitate to reprove the lazy even if others might overhear him.

Herbert thought the parson should also inquire about the kind of order that was kept within his parishioners' homes,

> as about prayers morning and evening on their knees, reading of
> Scripture, catechizing, singing of Psalms at their work and on holy
> days; who can read, who not; and sometimes he hears the children
> read himself and blesseth, encouraging also the servants to learn to
> read and offering to have them taught on holy-days by his servants.

The conscientious parson should not, according to Herbert, disdain "to enter into the poorest Cottage, though he even creep into it and though it smell never so loathsomely"—another reference to the unfortunate living conditions of many living in the countryside. In addition, the parson should comfort the sick or anyone "afflicted with loss of friend, or estate, or any ways distressed." In all respects, the parson should act, Herbert believed, as a father toward his parishioners, whether he was caring for their needs or dealing with their sins. Herbert would probably have agreed with the character in Shakespeare's *Henry VIII* who remarks that, ideally, "The churchman bears a bounteous mind indeed, / A hand as fruitful as the land that feeds us; / His dews fall every where" (1.3.55–57).

In every aspect of his own life and in the life of his community, the parson was God's representative in his parish, Herbert decreed, and he should behave accordingly. If he noticed someone being charitable to the poor, he should commend or reward that person in some way. If he noticed a person sinning, he should strive to correct such behavior rather than immediately turning the sinner over to the legal authorities. If, however, the sinful behavior was heinous or blatantly illegal, the parson should seek full punishment for the offender. "Thus both in rewarding virtue and punishing vice, the Parson endeavoureth to be in God's stead, knowing that Country people are drawn or led by sense more than by faith, by present rewards or punishments more than by future." Likewise, when catechizing his flock—that is, when teaching or reminding them of Christian truths by asking them questions— the parson should approach each person on his or her own level. Once, for instance, a parson asked a countryman what a miserable person should do. When the countryman was unsure of the proper answer, the parson

> asked him again, what he would do if he were in a ditch? This familiar illustration made the answer so plain that he [the countryman] was even ashamed of his ignorance; for he could not but say he would haste out of it as fast as he could. Then [the parson] proceeded to ask whether he could get out of the ditch alone, or whether he needed a helper, and [asked] who was that helper.

That helper, of course, was Christ, and Herbert's point is clear: Rural folk often needed to be taught in terms they could easily understand from their own practical experiences. The advantage of catechizing, Herbert notes, is that "at Sermons or Prayers men may sleep or wander; but when one is asked a question, he must discover what he is."

THE RURAL PARSON AS LAWYER AND DOCTOR

The parson's role in the local community, according to Herbert, went far beyond that of being a religious teacher. He should be a kind of "Lawyer also, and a Physician": "Therefore hee endures not that any of his Flock should go to Law, but in any Controversy they should resort to him as their Judge." Herbert knew, of course, that English people in all places and at all social levels were increasingly resorting to lawsuits and court cases whenever disputes arose, and so he expected his ideal country parson to be familiar with the law and skilled in resolving disagreements before they ever made it to court. However, "when ever any controversy is brought" to the parson, Herbert advised that the parson should never decide the case by himself but should send for "three or four of the ablest of the Parish to hear the cause with him, whom he makes to deliver their opinion first; out of which he gathers, in case he be ignorant himself, what to hold; and so the thing passeth with more authority and less envy." The parson, Herbert thought, should be concerned with absolute justice, so that if the poorest man of the parish stole merely a pin from the richest man, that pin should be restored absolutely. But as soon as the pin was restored, the parson should exhort the rich man to show charity.

Sometimes, of course, a dispute had to go to court: Sometimes the case was so serious or so complex, or the parties involved were so contentious, that there was no other option. Even in such cases, however, Herbert thought the parson should show the disputants "how to go to Law, even as Brethren and not as enemies, neither avoiding therefore one another's company, much less defaming one another." In comments such as this, Herbert offers a vivid sense of what day-to-day social life could be like in a small English village or town. Things were not always as harmonious as one might have hoped, but the churches and courts were two mechanisms for coping with any tensions that might arise.

Just as Herbert thought the country parson should function as a kind of lawyer, he also believed the parson should act as a kind of doctor:

> if there be any of his flock sick, he is their Physician, or at least his
> Wife, of whom instead of the qualities of the world he asks no other
> but to have the skill of healing a wound or helping the sick. But if
> neither himself nor his wife have the skill, and his means serve [that
> is, if he has enough money], he keeps some young practitioner in
> his house for the benefit of his Parish, whom yet he ever exhorts not
> to exceed his bounds [that is, go beyond his abilities], but in tickle
> [difficult or dangerous] cases to call in help. If all fail, then he keeps
> good correspondence with some neighbour Physician, and entertains
> [employs] him for the cure of his Parish.

These comments remind us how primitive and how rare health care could be in Shakespeare's era, especially for people living in the countryside. Yet Herbert seems confident that any reasonably intelligent person could learn many practical remedies by consulting standard books of the era, especially books about the proper use of various herbs. Herbert believed that God, by providing such useful plants, was the true physician. He felt that the ideal parson, in his duties as a kind of country doctor, should know "what herbs may be used in stead of drugs of the same nature," and he should also know how "to make the garden the shop. For home-bred medicines are both more easy for the parson's purse, and more familiar for all men's bodies." Herbert argued that the parson should use prayers as part of his treatments, but he also argued that the parson should never practice medicine so widely or so often that he took patients away from true physicians.

SINS OF THE COUNTRYSIDE

In keeping an eye on his flock, the country parson, according to Herbert, had to watch not only for obvious sins (such as adultery, murder, hatred, and lying) but also for less obvious infractions, such as gluttony or covetousness. These last two sins could easily overtake a person before he was even aware that his desires had become excessive. Sensible provision for one's family and future was one thing, according to Herbert, but hoarding and stinginess, especially if they meant mistreating one's servants, were another. Country people, he felt, should be generous with their neighbors and should not try to take advantage of one another, yet Herbert also thought that "Country-people are full of these petty injustices, being cunning to make use of another and spare themselves." He believed that the country parson should make sure his parishioners did not overeat or overindulge in alcohol in ways that damaged their physical or financial health or harmed the community. Any kind of excessive drinking or eating that made people incapable of work, for instance, should be discouraged. Surely Herbert would have disagreed with Falstaff when he says, in *2 Henry IV*, "If I had a thousand sons, the first humane principle I would teach them should be, to forswear thin potations and to addict themselves to sack [rich wine]" (4.3.122–25).

Alcohol discouraged proper work, according to Herbert, and encouraged idleness, which Herbert considered England's greatest cause of sin. "For when men have nothing to do, then they fall to drink, to steal, to whore, to scoff, to revile, to all sorts of gamings. Come, say they, we have nothing to do, let's go to the Tavern, or to the stews [whorehouses] or what not." Everyone therefore, according to Herbert, should either have a job or be preparing for one. Married men, in particular, should have their hands full, both as husbands and fathers and as managers of their own affairs. A married farmer, for instance, should be concerned with such matters as "improvement of his grounds, by drowning or draining, stocking or fencing, and ordering his land to the best advantage both of himself and his neighbours." But a married man's family and servants should be his chief concern, and he should "take as much joy in a straight-growing child or servant as a Gardener doth in a choice tree." Herbert remarks that if men could "find out this delight, they would seldom be from home; whereas now, of any place, they are least there." In comments such as this, we sense the inevitable distance in rural England between lofty ideals and everyday reality.

That social life in the country could be far from perfect led Herbert to give special praise to that most important of local law officers—the justice of the peace, an office once held by Shakespeare's father. Justices were agents of the monarch dispersed throughout the land, and so it is that Robert Shallow introduces himself in *2 Henry IV* as "one of the King's justices of the peace"

(3.2.58). Herbert considered a man's willingness to serve as a justice "an honourable Employment of a Gentle or Noble-man in the Country he lives in, enabling him with power to do good, and to restrain all those who else might both trouble him and the whole State." Herbert felt that all men who were wise and had good judgment were obligated to serve as justices and to seek such service. He admitted that sometimes the justices took bribes, were socially undistinguished, and faced unappealing tasks, but he thought these were all reasons why good and wise men should volunteer to serve.

RURAL RESPONSIBILITIES AND COUNTRY CUSTOMS

Herbert felt that socially prominent young countrymen who were heirs to their families' fortunes had special obligations to prepare themselves to run their households properly. They should not only follow the best examples set by their fathers but should also observe the best practices on other estates. In addition, they should read widely, especially in books about law. They should not be "truant[s] in the law," as one of Shakespeare's characters confesses himself to have been (*1 Henry VI* [2.4.7]). Rather they should attend local legal proceedings, not only out of respect to the judges but also to learn the practical aspects of the law. Heirs, Herbert believed, should learn as much as possible about England and should strive to serve in Parliament. When at home, they should also practice their military skills in case those should ever be needed. In the meantime, younger brothers in prominent families— that is, brothers who were not heirs (as Herbert himself was not)—should be properly employed and not waste their time in frivolous social activities such as "dressing, Complimenting, visiting and sporting" but should study such subjects as the civil law, mathematics, fortification, and navigation. If any "young Gallant" found such study boring, he should travel abroad, either to the American colonies or to the Continent and should make his life useful there.

Not all aspects of life in the country should involve hard work or strict religious devotion, Herbert stressed. Local customs of play and festivity should be respected, especially if they were "good and harmless," since "Country people are much addicted to them," so that for the parson "to favor them therein is to win their hearts, and to oppose them therein is to deject them." If there were anything bad about a local custom, the country parson should strive, Herbert believed, to pare that part of the apple away and leave the good parts. In particular, Herbert praised the important annual custom of walking the fields, celebrating the harvest, and sharing the harvest with the poor. Such shared activities helped, he felt, to breed love in the community, and anyone who regularly absented himself from such gatherings should, in Herbert's opinion, be rebuked. For the same reason, the country parson should encourage mutual hospitality among the people in his locale; dining and supping together could help patch up differences and promote social harmony.

Evidence of country customs survives from numerous other sources besides Herbert's book. These include Philip Stubbes's disapproving depiction of local celebrations. Stubbes, a strict Puritan, described how in spring

> or some other time of the year, every parish, town and village
> assemble themselves together, both men, women and children, old
> and young, even all indifferently; and either going all together or
> dividing themselves into companies, they go some to the woods
> and groves, some to the hills and mountains, some to one place and
> some to another, where they spend all the night in pleasure pastimes;
> and in the morning they return, bringing with them birch boughs
> and branches of trees, to deck their assemblies withal. . . . But their
> chiefest jewel they bring from thence is their May-pole, which they
> bring home with great veneration, as thus. They have twenty or forty
> yoke of oxen, every ox having a sweet nose-gay of flowers placed on
> the tip of his horns: and these oxen draw home this May-pole
> . . . which is covered all over with flowers and herbs, bound round
> about with strings from the top to the bottom, and sometime painted
> with variable colours, with two or three hundred men, women and
> children following it with great devotion. And thus being reared
> up with handkerchiefs and flags streaming on the top, they straw
> the ground about, bind green boughs about it, set up summer-halls,
> bowers, and arbors hard by it; and then they fall to banquet and feast,
> to leap and dance about it . . . .

Stubbes—a far less indulgent Christian than Herbert—considered such practices heathenish and even satanic and condemned the maypole as a "stinking idol." He was equally censorious of the custom of choosing a "Lord of Misrule" during the winter season, when

> all the wildheads of the parish, convening together, choose them a
> Grand-Captain (of all mischief) whom they ennoble with the title
> of My Lord of Misrule, and him they crown with great solemnity

FOLKLORE, SUPERSTITION, AND WITCHCRAFT

By the time Shakespeare was born, Christianity had been the official religion in England and in most of Europe for about a millennium, but by the early 1500s Christendom had begun to split seriously between Roman Catholic and Protestant factions. Alongside traditional religious beliefs, ancient folklore and superstition had long flourished, and in the sixteenth century witchcraft also became a matter of increasing discussion and sometimes even violent punishment. Supernatural beliefs of one sort or another, and in one combination or another, affected almost everyone in Shakespeare's period. Attitudes toward the beliefs of others—sometimes supportive, sometimes harshly critical—also affected the lives of Shakespeare and his contemporaries.

The folklore of Shakespeare's day often revolved around animals. Many people associated creatures such as bats, cats, and rats, among others, with negative legends, while birds such as cocks, pelicans, and robins often had highly positive associations. Plants were also the subject of specific popular beliefs: Mandrake plants, for instance, were believed by some to grow beneath the areas where criminals were hanged and were thought to scream when pulled from the ground. These types of superstitions were widespread in Shakespeare's England and often were endorsed by long communal tradition. Various rites, such as dancing around a maypole or walking as a group around the perimeters of a parish, aimed to promote fertility in people and in the local fields. Belief in ghosts, spirits, fairies, and magical powers were not uncommon, although skeptics also existed. People who believed in magic during this period (such as alchemists, who tried to turn "base" metals into gold) were often the forerunners of modern scientists, though some were cranks and charlatans intent on profiting from the credulity of others.

Worries about witches became increasingly common as the sixteenth century wore on. Witchcraft was an accusation that was easy to make and hard to disprove, and hundreds of people—mostly women—were tried, convicted, and executed for being witches during this time. Christianity was often in conflict with other supernatural systems of belief during this era, but often it helped support those other systems, as when witches were assumed to be agents of Satan or when ghosts were assumed to have been sent from hell.

"Hand in hand, with fairy grace,
Will we sing, and bless this place."
— *A Midsummer Night's Dream* (5.1.399–400)

and adopt for their king. This king anointed, chooseth forth twenty, thirty, threescore or a hundred lusty guts, like to himself, to wait upon his lordly majesty, and to guard his noble person. Then, every one of these his men, he investeth with liveries of green, yellow, or some other light wanton color; and as though they were not bawdy—gaudy enough I should say, they bedeck themselves with scarves, ribbons and laces hanged all over with gold rings, precious stones, and other jewels: this done, they tie about either leg twenty or forty bells, with rich handkerchiefs in their hands, and sometimes laid across their shoulders and necks, borrowed for the most part of their pretty Mopsies and loving Bessies, for bussing [kissing] them in the dark. Thus all things set in order, then have they their hobby-horses, dragons and other antics, together with their bawdy pipers and thundering drummers to strike up the devil's dance withal. Then march these heathen company towards the church and church-yard, their pipers piping, their drummers thundering, their stumps dancing, their bells jingling, their handkerchiefs swinging about their heads like madmen, their hobby-horses and other monsters skirmishing amongst the throng, and in this sort they go to the church (I say) and into the church (though the minister be at prayer or preaching) dancing and swinging their handkerchiefs, over their heads in the church, like devils incarnate, with such a confused noise, that no man can hear his own voice. Then, the foolish people they look, they stare, they laugh, they fleer, and mount upon forms and pews to see these goodly pageants solemnized in this sort. Then, after this, about the church they go again and again, and so forth into the church-yard where they have commonly their summer-halls, their bowers, arbors, and banqueting houses set up, wherein they feast, banquet and dance all that day and (peradventure) all the night too. And thus these terrestrial furies spend the Sabbath day.

Even allowing for some exaggeration on Stubbes's part, country celebrations could, paradoxically, often be both chaotic and well prepared, both uninhibited and carefully organized. Puritans such as Stubbes disdained these kinds of festivities, and even a country parson as tolerant as Herbert must have found some of these practices disturbing. Their existence, however, helps remind us that life in the villages, small towns, and countryside during Shakespeare's time could sometimes be quite exciting indeed.

Even the rituals directly related to rural existence could involve real joy, as the German traveler Paul Hentzner noted when reporting on his visit to England in 1598:

> As we were returning to our inn, we happened to meet some country people celebrating their Harvest Home. Their last load of corn [grain] they crown with flowers, having beside an image richly dressed, by which perhaps they would signify Ceres [the Roman goddess of grains]; this they keep moving about, while men and women, men and maidservants, riding through the streets in the carts, shout as loud as they can till they arrive at the barn.

Hentzner's reference to an "inn" is significant, because it implies the travel that often took place in Shakespeare's time from villages to towns, especially market towns, and also among various towns. As Hentzner's remarks also make clear, however, even the biggest towns in the England of this era were surrounded by fields and depended intimately on agriculture. This can easily be seen when looking at any of the splendid maps of the

A 1569 painting titled *A Marriage Feast at Bermondsey*. This painting depicts society during the reign of Elizabeth I of England. *(Joris Hoefnagel)*

counties of Britain included in John Speed's *The Theatre of the Empire of Great Britain*, first published in 1610–1611. When looking at Speed's bird's-eye views of English "cities," one is immediately struck by how small they seem, as well as by how few houses they contain and how much greenery they are both surrounded by and encompass. Fields full of grain, sheep, and other livestock were almost always within easy walking distance. The counties themselves were far from densely populated; most of the land consisted of fields, pastures, forests, and undeveloped tracts. Different counties were often known for different kinds of agricultural and manufactured products—barley in Bedfordshire, sheep in Buckinghamshire, minerals such as tin in Cornwall, and coal and iron in Derbyshire, to mention just four of the more than 60 places Speed depicts. Every county, though, depended in some way or another on agriculture, not only for its prosperity but for its very survival. So did the nation at large. In Shakespeare's England, the countryside was never far from any city, and that was true even of London—"proud London," as it is called by one of Shakespeare's characters (*2 Henry IV* [1.3.104]), the biggest city by far in England and the biggest city of this period in all of Europe.

Sources and Further Reading

Herbert, George. *The Temple and A Priest to the Temple*. London: Dent, 1908. Print.

Speed, John. *The Counties of Britain*. Intro. Nigel Nicolson; county commentaries by Alasdair Hawkyard. New York: Thames and Hudson, 1989. Print.

Tusser, Thomas. *A Hundreth Good Pointes of Husbandry*. 1557. London: Robert Triphook, 1810. Print.

Williams, Penry. *The Later Tudors: England, 1547–1603*. New York: Oxford University Press, 1995. Print.

DAILY LIFE IN LONDON

It is no exaggeration to say that in Shakespeare's England, all roads—or at least the most important ones—led to London. London was the capital city of the nation—a nation that now included Wales, as well as settlements in Ireland and a growing number of overseas colonies. But London was also the center of English commerce and foreign trade, just as it was the most important market for any produce raised or goods manufactured in the rest of the country. Serious legal business often had to be done in London, the site of most of the important courts of law, and London was also the seat of the royal court and the place where Parliament met. There were many reasons, then, for many people to visit London at least once in their lives and often far more frequently than that. This was especially true if they were economically, politically, or socially ambitious. Yet London was also often seen as a place where people unemployed in their own villages or towns might find jobs, and so much of the enormous growth in the city's population during Shakespeare's time was due to migration from other parts of the kingdom. London had always been an important city in English history, but in Shakespeare's day it had also become one of the largest and most important cities in all of Europe. Many a citizen of England must have felt as Davy feels in Shakespeare's play *2 Henry IV* when he says, "I hope to see London once ere I die" (5.3.60).

TRAVELING TO LONDON AND STAYING AT ENGLISH INNS

Getting to London was not especially easy. Complaints about the condition of the road system were proverbial. Paving in the modern sense was nonexistent, so the roads that did exist were often muddy and full of gaping holes. People in country parishes were expected to help maintain the condition of roads in their vicinities, but apparently they were not especially dedicated to this task. Thus a German visitor to England in 1592 wrote that "On the road we passed through a villainous boggy and wild country and several times missed our way because the country thereabout is very little inhabited and is nearly a waste; and there is one spot in particular where the mud is so deep that in my opinion it would scarcely be possible to pass with a coach in winter or in rainy weather." Travel, therefore, usually took place by foot or on horseback and could often take a long time, although Paul Hentzner, another German traveler in the late 1590s, rented a series of post horses on his journey toward London and expressed surprise at how swiftly they could run. Nevertheless, many people making their way toward London must have agreed with Touchstone in *As You Like It* when he said, "When I was at home, I was in a better place, but travellers must be content" (2.4.17–18).

Fortunately for anyone traveling, England was famous for the number and quality of its inns, not only in the larger towns and villages but especially

A map of London, published in 1653. The original map was printed in 1593. *(Map by John Norden)*

in London itself. William Harrison boasted that the "manner of harboring" in these inns was

> not like to that of some other countries, in which the host or
> goodman of the house doth challenge a lordly authority over his
> guests, but clean otherwise, sith [since] every man may use his inn
> as his own house in England, and have for his money how great or
> little variety of victuals and what other service himself shall think
> expedient to call for. Our inns are also very well furnished with
> napery; for beside the linen used at the tables, which is commonly
> washed daily, is such and so much as belongeth unto the estate and
> calling of the guest. Each comer is sure to lie in clean sheets.

Travelers who went by foot, according to Harrison, paid a penny a night to rent a room, whereas travelers with horses were allowed to stay in rooms rent free as there was a charge for boarding their horses. Harrison was proud that if a traveler were to lose anything "whilst he abideth in the inn, the host is bound by a general custom to restore the damage, so that there is no greater security anywhere for travelers than in the greatest inns of England." Conditions were not entirely ideal, however. Employees at the inns, especially those charged with caring for the horses or dispensing beer, could be deceptive and were often in league with local robbers, who would learn from employees at the inns about which travelers were carrying the most money or conveying the most goods. These travelers often would be robbed later on the roads, although rarely if ever in the inns themselves. Few such victims would have taken much comfort in the words that the Duke of Venice addresses to Desdemona's father in *Othello*: "The [person] robb'd that smiles steals something from the thief" (1.3.557).

Despite the ever-present possibility of being robbed while traveling in England, Harrison still boasted about the English inns: "In all our inns we have plenty of ale, beer, and sundry kinds of wine, and such is the capacity of some of them that they are able to lodge two hundred or three hundred persons and their horses at ease, and thereto with a very short warning make such provision for their diet as to him that is unacquainted withal may seem to be incredible." Harrison considered the inns in London the worst in the whole country (though others strongly disagreed with that appraisal), although he thought they were still "far better than the best that I have heard of in any foreign country." One recalls the words of a character in *1 Henry*

IV concerning one hazard of staying at an English inn: "I think this be the most villainous house in all London road for fleas: I am stung like a tench [a fish that appears to have small bites all over its body]" (2.1.14–15).

Harrison noted that innkeepers often competed vigorously with one another to offer the best possible "entertainment of their guests, as about fineness and change of linen, furniture [provision] of bedding, beauty of rooms, service at the table, costliness of plate, strength of drink, variety of wines, and well using of horses." Inns even competed in the "gorgeousness of their very signs at their doors." Harrison's good opinion of English inns was echoed several decades later by the much-traveled Fynes Moryson, who commented that "there is no place in the world where passengers may so freely command as in the English inns, and are attended for themselves and their horses as well as if they were at home, and perhaps better, each servant being ready at call, in hope of a small reward in the morning. Never did I see inns so well furnished with household stuff." Many a traveler newly arrived in London could have spoken the very words uttered by Antipholous of Syracuse in *The Comedy of Errors*:

> . . . I'll view the manners of the town,
> Peruse the traders, gaze upon the buildings,
> And then return and sleep within mine inn,
> For with long travel I am stiff and weary. (1.2.12–15)

LONDON'S CROWDED STREETS

After arriving in London and emerging from an inn after an evening's stay, what would a visitor find? Crowded streets, for one thing. London was brimming with people, and more were arriving each day from the countryside, intent on living there. They were walking and on horseback, and the many carts and carriages caused frequent "traffic jams." Thomas Dekker reported in 1606 that

> In every street, carts and coaches make such a thundering as if the world ran upon wheels: at every corner, men, women and children meet in such shoals, that posts are set up of purpose to strengthen the houses, lest with jostling one another they should shoulder them down. Besides, hammers are beating in one place, tubs hooping in another, pots clinking in a third, water-tankards [carts to carry water] running at tilt in a fourth. Here are porters sweating under burdens,

there merchants' men bearing bags of money. Chapmen [merchants] (as if they were at leap-frog) skip out of one shop into another. Tradesmen (as if they were dancing galliards) are lusty at legs and never stand still.

Similarly, in 1617 Fynes Moryson also commented on the congestion, noting that "Sixty or seventy years ago coaches were very rare in England, but at this day pride is so far increased, as there be few gentlemen of any account (I mean elder brothers) who have not their coaches, so as the streets of London are almost stopped with them." To make matters worse, most of the streets were, in the words of Baron Waldstein (a Moravian visitor in 1600), "dark and narrow." This did not prevent Waldstein, like most visitors to London, from being highly impressed with the burgeoning English capital.

LONDON BRIDGE

The ancient stone walls that had long encircled the city could not contain the growing population, and so what German traveler Hentzner called "very extensive suburbs" had long been springing up outside the walls and especially across the mighty River Thames, which was central to the rapid growth of this city. One way to cross the river was to use the famous and impressive London Bridge, which no longer exists. Hentzner described it as "a bridge of stone eight hundred feet in length, of wonderful work; it is supported upon twenty piers of square stone, sixty feet high, and thirty broad, joined by arches of about twenty feet diameter. The whole is covered on each side with houses, so disposed, as to have the appearance of a continued street, not at all of a bridge." Hentzner also noted that the south end of the bridge featured "a tower, on whose top the heads of such as have been executed for high treason are placed on iron spikes: we counted above thirty." Contemporary depictions of the bridge often feature views of these spiked heads grimacing down at the travelers below. Baron Waldstein likewise noted the heads, but he also commented on the bridge's "amazingly skillful construction" and its "extremely fine buildings." He considered it "easily one of the finest bridges in the whole of Europe, both for size and for beauty."

Fynes Moryson was similarly impressed, calling the bridge "worthily to be numbered among the miracles of the world" as a work of ingenious construction. He noted that the "houses built upon the bridge" were "as great and high as those of the firm land, so as a man cannot know that he passeth a bridge, but would judge himself to be in the street, save that the houses

Old London Bridge, 1796. *(Joseph Mallord William Turner)*

on both sides are combined in the top, making the passage somewhat dark, and that some few open places the river of Thames may be seen on both sides." Donald Lupton, another contemporary observer, likewise admired the bridge, noting the loud noises that would emanate from beneath as the tidal flow of the Thames rose and receded and noting as well that anyone of any rank could cross the bridge or travel by boat beneath it. The bridge saved many people the costs of crossing the river by boat, and Lupton also observed that the incessant flow of the water beneath it meant that the bridge had to be kept in repair. Poor people used the bridge to lower buckets into the river to retrieve water, thus saving themselves the expense of paying to have water carried to their houses. Lupton concluded by praising the bridge as a structure "without compare, being [simultaneously] a dainty street, and a strong and most stately bridge." The existence of the bridge was crucial to the prosperity of the city, and so it is hardly surprising that a rebel in one of Shakespeare's plays proposes to "set London bridge on fire" as a way of furthering the success of his revolt (*2 Henry VI* [4.6.14]).

BOATING AND FISHING ON THE RIVER THAMES

The bridge was hardly the only way to cross the Thames. Most visitors to London, as well as many local residents, took advantage of the numerous ferryboats that regularly plied the waters. These boats, which were operated by several thousand "watermen," carried passengers across the river and up and down its banks, in much the same way that taxis shuttle people around large cities today. The boats were often attractive, but the men who operated them were known for loudly seeking customers and for being somewhat surly if they thought their tips too small. Sir Thomas Overbury considered the watermen aggressive businessmen and regular sources of lies and gossip, and he joked that they regarded London Bridge as a "most terrible eye-sore" since it robbed them of potential business. William Harrison estimated there were "two thousand wherries and small boats, whereby three thousand poor watermen are maintained through the carriage and recarriage of such persons as pass or repass from time to time" upon the river, and he also noted the existence of "huge tide-boats, tiltboats and barges, which either carry passengers or bring necessary provision" into the city.

One Italian visitor noted that people used the boats not only "to cross the river" but also "to enjoy themselves in the evenings." He claimed, "It is just as pleasant as it is to go in summertime along the grand canal in Venice," partly because traveling by river gave "a very fine view of beautiful palaces and gardens," so that "many boats [went] there for pleasure." Another foreign visitor reported that "a number of tiny streets lead to the Thames from both ends of the town; the boatmen wait there in great crowds, each one eager to catch [a customer], for all [potential passengers] are free to choose the ship they find most attractive and pleasing, while every boatman has the privilege on arrival of placing his ship to best advantage for people to step into." This same visitor also reported that some boats offered "charmingly upholstered and embroidered cushions laid across the seats, very comfortable to sit on or lean against," and "generally speaking the benches only seat two people next to one another. Many of [the boats] are covered in, particularly in rainy weather or fierce sunshine. They are extremely pleasant to travel in and carry one or a couple of boatmen."

Swans also abounded on the river and often took food from the hands of people in the boats. Hentzner, the German traveler, commented on the "immense number of swans, who wander up and down the river for some miles, in great security, nobody daring to molest, much less kill any of them, under penalty of a considerable fine." Elsewhere he noted that the Thames "abounds in swans, swimming in flocks: the sight of them and their noise, is vastly agreeable to the fleets that meet them in their course." Many a Londoner must have seen the same sight as a character in *3 Henry VI* who claimed to have watched "a swan / With bootless labor swim against the tide / And spend her strength with over-matching waves" (1.4.18–20).

Fishermen also plied the Thames each day. Harrison boasted of the "fat and sweet salmons daily taken in this stream" and of the many other fish, such as "barbells, trouts, chevins, perches, smelts, bream, roach, dace, gudgeon, and flounders" the river afforded. Unfortunately, nets that had been stretched beneath the river to catch fish often caused problems for the numerous boats. Hentzner reported that the Thames was "everywhere spread with nets for taking salmon and shad," and civil authorities often complained about the difficulties these nets created. Somehow, though, the river successfully accommodated a variety of bustling activities, and when it occasionally froze over, it became the scene of winter carnivals and impromptu ice-skating. Yet for most of the year the Thames was also a convenient place to dump sewage and garbage, and it is in this connection that Shakespeare seems to have thought of it most often, as when Falstaff, in *The Merry Wives of Windsor*, speaks of being "carried in a basket like a barrow of butcher's offal, . . . to be thrown in the Thames" (3.5.4–6). It was across the Thames that most people came to witness the plays performed by Shakespeare's company at the Globe Theatre, which was located not in London but in the southern suburb of Southwark, just across the river from the capital city.

ST. PAUL'S CATHEDRAL AND PAUL'S WALK

Perhaps the most impressive building inside the city of London was St. Paul's Cathedral, which had existed in its present form since the early fourteenth century. Its steeple had been struck and burned away by lightning in 1561, and the structure of the rest of the building was often in poor repair, but the cathedral was still an imposing sight, both within and without. One visitor, for instance, called it "large and remarkable," while Hentzner was impressed by its "vastness and magnificence" and reported in detail on the imposing, elaborately inscribed tombs it contained, especially one "magnificent monument, ornamented with pyramids of marble and alabaster." He noted that the cathedral had "a very fine organ, which, at evening prayer, accompanied with other instruments, is delightful." Intrepid visitors then, as today, could climb to the top of the building, but in those days it was even possible to walk out onto the lead-covered roof. One visitor commented that "every

Sunday many men and women stroll together on this roof," and he reported that "Up there I had a splendid view of the entire city of London, of how long and narrow it is."

Illustration of "Paul's Walk" from William Harrison Ainsworth's *Old St. Paul's*, published by Chapman and Hall in 1841. *(John Franklin)*

Most of the walking, however, occurred up and down the nave (or central aisle) inside the cathedral. "Paul's walk" became a notorious place where people of all sorts congregated and strolled for all kinds of reasons, not all of them savory. Thomas Dekker, in a memorable and often satiric description, depicted the walk as a place full of "the daily sound and echo of much knavish villainy," including the work of pickpockets and other deceptive characters trying "by some sleight to cheat the poor country client [visiting London on legal business] of his full purse that is stuck under his girdle." Young country gentlemen visiting London were sometimes first befriended at Paul's and then later cheated or robbed, when drunk, at nearby taverns. Usury was practiced in the aisles of Paul's, and Dekker becomes especially indignant when he asks rhetorically,

> What swearing is there, yea, what swaggering, what facing and
> outfacing? What shuffling, what shouldering, what jostling, what
> jeering, what biting of thumbs to beget quarrels, what holding up of
> fingers to remember drunken meetings, what braving with feathers
> [in hats], what bearding with moustaches, what casting open of cloaks
> to publish new clothes, . . . so that when I hear such trampling up and
> down, such spitting, such hawking and such humming (every man's
> lips making a noise, yet not a word to be understood), I verily believe
> [the cathedral to be] the Tower of Babel newly . . . builded up.

It is difficult to read the reference to the "biting of thumbs to beget quarrels" and *not* think of the opening scene of Shakespeare's *Romeo and Juliet* ("Do you bite your thumb at us, sir? [1.1.44]). One wonders if Shakespeare may actually have witnessed such behavior in the center aisle at Paul's.

John Earle, like Dekker, also emphasized the sound inside the cathedral, describing it as resembling that of "bees, a strange humming or buzz, mixed of walking, tongues and feet. It is a kind of still roar or loud whisper." He called the walk "the great exchange of all discourse" and noted there was "no business whatsoever but is here stirring and afoot." He particularly considered the walk a den of thieves and pickpockets and called it a place where men resorted after first visiting "plays, tavern, and a bawdy-house," when they still had some "oaths left to swear." St. Paul's was a place where people met, did business, exchanged gossip, and came to see and be seen. Shakespeare, in *2 Henry IV*, alludes to the fact that servants (not always well qualified) could be hired at St. Paul's (1.2.52), and much else could be purchased there. Religious services were conducted in the cathedral and sermons were delivered both inside and outside, but for much of each day and much of every week St. Paul's was perhaps the most important social hub of the city.

A CITY OF CHURCHES AND SHOPS

St. Paul's was only the most massive and important of the capital's churches. London was filled with houses of worship, as a glance at any contemporary map will show. The spires of more than 100 churches were visible, and a church was usually at the social and spiritual center of every individual neighborhood or parish. Londoners worshipped in churches, were married and buried there, listened to sermons there, and had their children christened there. The church was one of the key places where neighbors were likely to meet regularly. Membership in a local church, as well as regular attendance there, was not only common but was also expected, and few Londoners failed to oblige. The Christian religion and its many neighborhood churches were central to their lives, and questions and disputes about religion were central to their minds and their politics.

Inevitably, Londoners also had to be concerned not only with the states of their souls but also with making practical livings. Isabella Whitney, in a lengthy poem from this era, gives a vivid sense of the various ways in which they did so and of the various streets and neighborhoods in which they operated. Thus she associated Watling Street and Canwick Street with the sale of fish and wool, and she linked Friday Street to the sale of linen. Various kinds of fancy clothing were sold at the Royal Exchange, while such items as knives, combs, and glass could be purchased not far from the Exchange at a market known as the "Stocks." Hosiery was available, according to Whitney, in Birchin Lane; boots and shoes were on sale in St. Martin's Street; while beds could be purchased in an area of the city known as Cornwall. The best tailors for women had shops near the church of St. Mary-le-Bow, although Whitney noted that tailors for both sexes "In every lane you some shall find / can do indifferent well." Weapons of various kinds were readily available, especially in Fleet Street or near the Tower of London, while Whitney noted that "For salt, oatmeal, candles, soap, / or what you else do want, / In many places shops are full," and she reported that wine was especially plentiful in a section of London known as Steelyard.

THE LIVERY COMPANIES

Many of the businesses mentioned by Whitney were overseen by the famous "livery companies" of London, whose leaders were expected to dress in distinctive kinds of clothing, or liveries. These companies were extremely important to the economy of the capital, and the halls of the various companies were scattered throughout the city. Liza Picard, in her immensely valuable book on Elizabethan London, notes that there were almost 100 of these companies or professional associations during Shakespeare's era, and some were particularly influential. Just as one could hardly walk far without encountering a church in London, so one could barely walk a great distance without coming across one of the halls of these various kinds of tradesmen or merchants.

Just to the west of St. Paul's Cathedral was the Stationers Hall—headquarters of the Elizabethan publishing industry. Not far to the south of the cathedral lay the hall of the Woodmongers, which was just a little west of Blacksmiths Hall. Slightly to the east and north of the cathedral lay Saddlers Hall, and to the north of that lay Goldsmiths Hall, Haberdashers Hall, and Plasterers Hall. Eastward, down Cheapside Street, lay Mercers Hall, which in turn was not far from Grocers Hall. To the north of those buildings were such other establishments as Bakers Hall, Weavers Hall, Girdlers Hall, and Armourers Hall. As one walked farther east on Cheapside Street, that thoroughfare turned into Poultry Street, and several blocks to the south of this intersection lay Cutlers Hall, Tallow Chandlers Hall, Skinners Hall, and Inn Holders Hall. Farther east (up Three Needle Street) lay Merchant Taylors Hall, while farther east yet, located on various streets, lay Leathersellers Hall, Bricklayers Hall, Pewterers Hall, Ironmongers Hall, and Clotherworkers Hall. Farther south, on the way to the river, lay Butchers Hall and Bakers Hall, while close to the river itself (on or near Thames Street) lay Fishmongers Hall, Dyers Hall, Joiners Hall, and Vintners Hall. A walk around London thus brought one close not only to many churches but also to the headquarters of various important businesses or industries. Members of the various companies, who constituted a large proportion of London's population, were probably not amused by Autolycus's comment in *The Winter's Tale*, "Let me have no lying. It becomes none but tradesmen" (4.4.722–23).

As Picard notes, many of the livery companies had existed since the 1100s, and there was hardly a single feature of life in London that was not affected by one of these highly important groups. Even a partial listing of them provides a sense of how diverse the economy of the city was—how many different ways a person might make a living. Membership in the livery companies, however, was not simply a smart business move but also involved becoming part of a smaller community of people who shared a common interest. Each livery company constituted a kind of subcommunity within the larger city of London. Each had its own hierarchy, its own set of rules and traditions, and its own set of occasional conflicts and tensions. At the lowest level of the hierarchy were the apprentices. As J. A. Sharpe notes, these were young people, usually boys, whose parents placed them (often at around age 14) with "masters" in various trades. The apprentices usually lived and worked in the households of their masters for seven years, learning appropriate skills and preparing for the day when they would demonstrate their mastery of the trade or craft practiced by their particular company.

Ideally, apprenticeship was intended not only to train future workers but also to impose discipline on young people who might otherwise prove unruly. Kathy Lynn Emerson notes that apprentices were prohibited from marrying or having premarital sex and they were supposed to avoid taverns and gambling. Apprentices were often well treated by their masters, who functioned in effect as substitute parents, but sometimes they were not, and punishments could be severe. Picard estimates that nearly half of all apprentices quit before their period of service was up, striking out on their own in the villages or small towns from which many of them had originally come. Those who managed to stick out the period of training and satisfy the requirements of the company became "journeymen" who worked for a daily wage, or they could establish shops of their own. Such people were considered "freemen" of the city of London. This was an important status since, as Picard notes, only freemen could buy property in the city. She suggests that well over half of the male citizens of London had served time as apprentices, and a greater percentage were affiliated with one of the livery companies. Some men rose to quite high rank within their companies and became among the most prominent of London citizens.

The companies assisted their members in various ways, particularly through generous loans, and members often married the daughters or widows of other members. Company courts helped mediate disputes among members, and the companies often provided charity for widows and poorer (often older) members. When wealthier members died, they often left generous bequests to the companies in their wills. For all the people—husbands, wives, children, widows, and single men or boys—affiliated with a company at whatever level, the company or guild provided one of the most important of all social networks in London. Affiliation with a company was one of the surest forms of social security in highly insecure times. John of Gaunt, in *Richard III*, calls God "the widow's champion and defense" (1.2.43), but in

Elizabethan London, God often exercised his charity by working through the various companies.

Not all residents of London were lucky enough to be affiliated with a company. Many people earned livings by making or selling merchandise independently, or doing both, and women in particular could earn money by spinning wool or knitting. Women were often employed as domestic servants, usually beginning such service as teenagers and typically living in the homes of their employers, who provided wages, food, and clothing. The many wealthy people, including aristocrats, who owned large homes in London needed both male and female servants, but even people in the trades could often afford to employ a single servant, or sometimes several, in their more modest houses. Service in the homes of tradesmen or in the grand houses of the wealthy provided another of the various kinds of community (such as membership in livery companies or membership in parish churches) that helped insulate many Londoners—as well as citizens of other towns and villages—from social isolation and loneliness. Service was one of the many ways in which the life of a citizen could be structured, supervised by others, and given some degree of economic security.

INSIDE LONDON'S HOMES: FURNITURE AND MEALS

Inside the multistory homes of the more prosperous residents of Elizabethan London the walls were often painted or papered. Sometimes they were hung with tapestries or embroiderings or—less expensively—with painted cloths. Often these wall decorations contained moralistic messages or allegorical scenes, particularly dealing with biblical topics. In the homes of the wealthier citizens, family portraits were common, sometimes mounted on wood paneling. Carpets were still rare and were most likely to be found in the homes of the rich, whereas the wooden floors in most Elizabethan houses were covered with rushes (the stems of plants), straw, matting (particularly mats made from rushes), or even sand. Rushes were changed only rarely; instead, new rushes were placed on top of the old. Not surprisingly, fleas were common in even the best homes and helped contribute to the spread of plague. Many houses tended to be damp and somewhat dark; windows, as Kathy Lynn Emerson notes, were still often made of oiled paper, although glass windows were becoming more common by the turn of the century. Candles and fireplaces provided additional light and heat, respectively, but even the best residences tended to be somewhat cold in the winter.

DISEASE

Sickness and disease of all sorts were common in Shakespeare's England, partly because living conditions were so unsanitary and partly because medicine was neither very advanced nor widely available. Humans lived close to their own filth and the filth of animals to a degree that is hard to imagine today, and thus opportunities for infection were many. We now know, for instance, that the constant and deadly epidemics of "plague" that struck England throughout this period resulted from the bites of fleas living on infected rats, but people at the time tended to attribute such outbreaks to bad air and even to the wrath of God. The only effective way to avoid the plague during these times was to flee from infected areas—an option available mainly to the wealthy—although authorities also tried quarantining infected households, which often resulted in even more deaths.

Many kinds of sickness were explained as resulting from imbalances in the four basic "humors" of the body (blood, phlegm, black bile, and yellow bile). Treatment of such imbalance could include changes in diet but often involved "bleeding" the patient. In general, people of Shakespeare's era had to endure much more pain and suffering than is common today. There were no wonder drugs such as aspirin, no antibiotics, and no effective anesthetics. People of this era knew that death might strike at any time, and they also knew that their lives were likely to be far briefer than anything we are accustomed to today. Thus they focused more on matters of religion and a possible afterlife (for good or for bad) than modern people tend to do.

"Diseases desperate grown
By desperate appliance are reliev'd,
Or not at all."
— *Hamlet* (4.3.9–11)

The dark, drafty interiors were just two of many conditions that encouraged people to go to bed earlier than tends to be the custom today.

Furniture in Elizabethan homes was sparse. Most of it was made of wood (often oak), and very little of it was upholstered. When Elizabethans ate meals, most members of the household sat on benches or stools on either side of a table that was often a board placed on top of trestles. Such boards could be taken down at the end of a meal and set against a wall. At one end of the board, the most important member of the household—typically the husband and father or some other dominant male—would usually sit in the only chair (hence our modern phrase *chairman of the board*).

Shakespearova studovna.

William Shakespeare, od K. Winklera.

Shakespearovo rodiště.

Portrait of William Shakespeare underneath depictions of his study (top left) and birthplace (top right) from an April 1864 edition of *Zlatá Praha* magazine.

Breakfast, which was eaten early and often quickly, if at all, usually consisted of bread, beer, and perhaps some meat. Everyone, including children, drank beer, ale, and wine, which were safer to drink than untreated water, and the heavy consumption of alcohol, beginning at breakfast, must have affected (for good or bad) the general mood of the population. Surely the sentiments expressed in the following lyric were not uncommon:

> I love no roast but a nut-brown toast,
>   And a crab laid in the fire;
> A little bread shall do me stead,
>   Much bread I not desire;
> No frost nor snow, no wind I trow [believe],
>   Can hurt me if I would,
> I am so wrapped and thoroughly lapped
>   Of jolly good ale and old.

Around noon, Elizabethans had "dinner," typically the most substantial daily meal, especially for anyone who could afford it. Of the poorest folk, Harrison remarked that "they generally dine and sup when they may, so that to talk of their order of repast it were but a needless matter." The middling sort, however, could often dine quite well, and the higher up the social hierarchy one progressed, the better the meals would be. Walter Besant, the great historian of London life throughout the centuries, notes that in the Tudor period the more elaborate dinners—especially any hosted by the livery companies—were often

plentiful and varied. A salad was served first, then the beef and mutton; next fowls, and fish; game followed, woodcock being the most plentiful; and pastry and sweets came last. Honey was poured over the meat. The most important part of the meal, however, was the "banquet" or dessert which followed: at this part of the dinner an amazing quantity of sweetmeats was taken; for this everyone adjourned to another room in winter; to the garden in summer.

In the winter fresh meat was not always to be had: most people laid in large quantities of beef in October or November, which they salted. The markets, however, made up for the absence of fresh meat by the abundance of all kinds of birds which were brought into London; they were trapped, or shot with sling and stone, in the marshes along the lower reaches of the Thames. Pork could be had all the year round. Fresh fish was generally plentiful, but it was sometimes dear [expensive]. At such times the people fell back upon stockfish, which was often bad and the cause of much disease.

Herrings were brought by sea from Yarmouth in barrels, and partly salted, as they are at this day. They were a favorite form of food, and were made into pasties highly spiced.

Not everyone ate dinners as substantial as the ones Besant describes here, but for almost everyone, dinner was indeed the most substantial meal of the day. Thus Evans, in *The Merry Wives of Windsor*, announces, "I will make an end of my dinner; There's pippins [apples] and cheese to come" (1.2.11–13).

Even later, another meal—"supper"—was served around six or seven, if not earlier. Here again, meat and fish were popular sources of protein, as was cheese. As Jeffrey Singman and many other sources comment, meat was more common in English diets than on the continent, at least among those who could afford it. William Harrison noted that

> there is no restraint of any meat, either for religion's sake or public order, in England, but it is lawful for every man to feed upon whatsoever he is able to purchase, except it be upon those days whereon eating of flesh is especially forbidden by laws of the realm, which order is taken only to the end [that] our numbers of cattle may be the better increased and that abundance of fish which the sea yieldeth more generally received.

Yet whatever they ate, as Kathy Lynn Emerson notes, people used their fingers (along with knives to spear food) far more typically in Shakespeare's era than is the custom today. Forks did not become common in England until nearly 1700. The traveler Fynes Moryson, in fact, was puzzled when he noticed that the typical Italian could not "endure by any means to have his dishes touched by fingers, seeing that all men's fingers are not alike clean." Elizabethans tried to solve this problem by washing their hands before eating, and some tables even featured finger bowls full of water.

A container of salt would also have been on most tables, since salt was popular in the English diet. Many meats and fishes were salty to begin with, having often been preserved in salt (or sometimes by smoking), but sweet tastes were provided by fruits and honey, and vegetables also helped round out the diet. Fruits and vegetables might be grown in family gardens, even in London, or could be bought at local markets. Other kinds of spices were used to counteract the taste of too much salt, although such spices—often imported from abroad and therefore somewhat expensive—would have been more common in wealthier homes. Eating was preceded by the saying of grace and sometimes ended with the same ritual—another indication of the importance of religion in the typical Elizabethan home. Sometimes, Emerson notes, food was served on thick slices of bread on top of wooden "trenchers," although increasingly the wooden plates were used alone or were replaced by plates made of pewter or, among the wealthy, of even finer metals.

Most Londoners spent their days doing work of some sort, either in their shops if they were merchants or craftsmen or in their homes if they were women. Furthermore, wives often assisted their husbands in running the family businesses. Not everyone, however, spent each and every day working. "After dinner," wrote the dramatist Thomas Dekker, "every man as his business leads him, some to dice, some to drabs [prostitutes], some to plays, some to take up money in the city, some to lend testers [coins] in Paul's [the aisles of St. Paul's Cathedral]." Some people visited taverns and others shopped, but most worked to support themselves and their families in some fashion.

However a Londoner was employed—whether working for himself, working for someone else, or not working much at all—the highlight of the evening was supper. After supper, some people walked for exercise; others socialized in taverns; and children often played games in the streets. Thomas Dekker has left a memorably satiric picture of the evening activities of some Londoners:

> The damasked-coated citizen, that sat in his shop both forenoon and afternoon, and looked more sourly on his poor neighbors than if he had drunk a quart of vinegar at a draught, sneaks out of his own doors and slips into a tavern where, either alone or with some other that battles [combine] their money together, they so ply themselves with penny pots, which, like small-shot, go off, pouring into their fat paunches, that at length they have not an eye to see withal, nor a good leg to stand upon. In which pickle, if any of them happen to be jostled down by a post [message carrier], that in spite of them will take the wall [walk closest to the walls of buildings facing streets and thus farthest from the streets themselves], and so reels them into the kennel [the gutter], who takes them up or leads them home? . . .
>
> Tush, this is nothing! Young shopkeepers that have but newly ventured upon the pikes of marriage, who are every hour showing

their wares to their customers, plying their business all day harder than Vulcan does his anvil, and seem better husbands than fiddlers that scrape for a poor living both day and night, . . . [often in the evenings go to taverns and] fall roundly to play the London prize, and that's at three several weapons, drinking, dancing, and dicing: their wives lying all that time in their beds sighing like widows, which is lamentable; the giddy-brained husbands wasting the portion they had with them, which once lost, they are (like maidenheads) never recoverable.

Dekker suggests that many of these young, abandoned wives found other men to keep them company in bed while their husbands were out gambling, but how common a practice this was is hard to determine. Leontes in *The Winter's Tale* remarks that "many a man there is, even at this present, / Now, while I speak this, holds his wife by th'arm, / That little thinks she has been sluiced in's absence, / And his pond fished by his next neighbor, by / Sir Smile, his neighbor" (1.2.190–96).

By the time darkness fell, however, most people were probably preparing themselves for bed and sleep. Public baths existed, but bathing, for most people, usually took place in large wooden tubs situated in front of fires. "Bathrooms" in the modern sense did not exist in most homes, nor did toilets or commodes except in a few rare cases. "Chamber pots" were still the primary method of relieving oneself when inside one's house, especially at night, and were often placed under beds. "Close stools" (stools with pans beneath them) were more expensive but also more comfortable, as they made it easier to sit while urinating or defecating. Disposal of waste was always a problem, especially in ever-growing London. The streets were often filthy with the waste of animals—especially horses and pigs—but also of humans, and inevitably much of this filth made it into the local streams and rivers, particularly the Thames. Much of the garbage generated by a London household was eaten by scavenging animals and birds, such as pigs, crows, and hawklike "kites." The smell of London and of Londoners must often have been quite ripe, both inside and outside the home. Deodorants as such did not exist, but perfumes of various sorts were frequently and often heavily applied. Falstaff, in *The Merry Wives of Windsor*, speaks of being hidden inside a basket of dirty clothes—a basket full of "foul shirts and smocks, socks, foul stockings, greasy napkins, [so] that . . . there was the rankest compound of villainous smell that ever offended nostril" (3.5.90–

93). Clothes were often washed in the local rivers and wells, one of many reasons those sources of water were less fresh than would have been ideal.

When Londoners did go to sleep, the quality of their beds depended on the sizes of their incomes. Wealthy Londoners could afford fairly elaborate beds, with substantial headboards, rich carvings, and attractive curtains, although the less wealthy had to be content with less elaborate accommodations. In general, though, there was a steady improvement in bedding for all classes during this period. Harrison notes that in the recent past English people had been accustomed to lie "full often upon straw pallets, on rough mats covered only with a sheet, under coverlets made of dogswain [a coarse woolen fabric] or hapharlots [rough, shaggy cloth]" with often only "a good round log under their heads instead of a bolster or pillow." Within seven years of marriage, a man in the recent past might hope to be able to purchase "a mattress or flock-bed [stuffed with wool or cotton], and thereto a sack of chaff to rest his head upon," in which case he might consider himself "as well lodged as the lord of the town."

Pillows, Harrison reports, had recently been considered appropriate "only for women in childbed," while servants had often been lucky simply to have sheets to sleep with. By the late sixteenth century, bedding had generally improved for most people, particularly in London and other towns, and mattresses stuffed with feathers were becoming increasingly common. Even so, many people (especially servants) still slept on modest "truckle beds," which could be moved about on wheels, and many people—not just husbands and wives—shared beds and slept together in the same rooms. Children often slept with their parents; siblings often shared beds with one another; and servants (although sexually segregated) often occupied the same beds. With the advent of tobacco, many Londoners smoked pipes before going to sleep, although smoking could also take place at practically any other time of the day. Perhaps the last thing that most Londoners did before going to sleep each night was to say their prayers. Perhaps some of the tavern haunters described by Dekker said (or at least should have said) the following prayer, which was published in 1585:

O Lord my God, I wandered have
    As one that runs astray,
And have in thought, in word, and deed
    In idleness and play,
Offended sore thy Majesty,

In heaping sin to sin,
And yet thy mercy hath me spar'd,
So gracious hast thou been!

Many Elizabethan Londoners must have slept soundly, if only because of all the beer, wine, and ale they had consumed throughout the day, not to mention their often heavy meals, frequently dedicated work, and various extracurricular activities. After all (as Belarius remarks in *Cymbeline*), "weariness / Can snore upon the flint, when resty sloth / Finds the down pillow hard" (3.6.33–35).

HOW LONDONERS DRESSED

When Londoners awoke in the morning and began to dress for a new day, what kinds of clothes did they wear? Much depended on their incomes and on their varied places in the social hierarchy. Much also depended on the particular year and decade in which they happened to dress, for fashions, especially at the upper end of the social scale, were often in flux. Thus William Harrison condemned "the fantastical folly of our nation, even from the courtier to the carter," since he claimed that "no form of apparel liketh [pleases] us longer than the first garment is in the wearing, if it continue so long and be not laid aside to receive some other trinket newly devised by the fickle-headed tailors, who covet to have several tricks in cutting, thereby to draw fond [foolish] customers to more expense of money." At one moment, Harrison claimed, Spanish styles of dress might be in fashion and at the next moment French, or German, or even Turkish. "And as these fashions are diverse," he continued, "so likewise it is a world to see the costliness and the curiosity, the excess and the vanity, the pomp and the bravery, the change and the variety, and finally, the fickleness and the folly that is in all degrees [all social classes], insomuch that nothing is more constant in England than inconstancy of attire." Harrison claimed almost to feel sorry for tailors: "How many times must it [an article of clothing] be sent back again to him that made it! What chafing, what fretting, what reproachful language doth the poor workman bear away!" Thus York in *Richard II* comments on "fashions in proud Italy, / Whose manners still our tardy, apish nation / Limps after in base imitation" (2.1.21–23).

Much the same impression of the fickleness of English fashion is given by the Puritan satirist Philip Stubbes, whose famous *Anatomie of Abuses*

creates a memorable—if probably exaggerated—picture of women's fashions up and down the social hierarchy:

> Their Gowns be no less famous also; for some are of silk, some of velvet, some of grogram, some of taffata, some of scarlet, and some of fine cloth, of ten, twenty, or forty shillings a yard. But if the whole gown be not silk or velvet, then the same shall be laid with lace, two or three fingers broad, all over the gown, or else the most part. Or, if not so (as lace is not fine enough sometimes), then it must be guarded [ornamented] with great guards [trimmings] of velvet, every guard four or six fingers broad at the least, and edged with costly lace; and as these gowns be of diverse and sundry colors, so are they of diverse fashions, changing with the Moon, for some be of the new fashion, some of the old, some of this fashion, and some of that, some with sleeves hanging down to their skirts, trailing on the ground, and cast over their shoulders, like Cow-tails.
>
> Some have sleeves much shorter, cut up the arm, drawn out with diverse and sundry colors and pointed with silk-ribbons very gallantly, tied with true-loves knots (for so they call them).
>
> Some have Capes reaching down to the middest of their backs, faced with Velvet, or else with some fine wrought silk Taffata at the least, and fringed about very bravely [handsomely]; & (to shut up all in a word) some are pleated & crested down the back wonderfully, with more knacks than I can declare. Then have they petticoats of the best cloth that can be bought, and of the fairest dye that can be made. And sometimes they are not of cloth neither, for that is thought too base, but of scarlet, grograin [grogram], taffata, silk and such like, fringed about the skirts with silk fringe of changeable color. But which is more vain, of whatsoever their petticoats be, yet must they have kirtles (for so they call them), either of silk, velvet, grograin, taffata, satin, or scarlet, bordered with guards, lace, fringe, and I cannot tell what besides. So that when they have all these goodly robes upon them, women seem to be the smallest part of themselves, not natural women . . . so far hath this canker of pride eaten into the body of the commonwealth, that every poor Yeoman his Daughter, every Husbandman his daughter, & every Cottager his Daughter, will not spare to flaunt it out in such gowns, petticoats, & kirtles as these. And not withstanding that their Parents owe a brace of hundred

pounds more than they are worth, yet will they have it, *quo iure quave iniuria*, either by hook or crook, by right or wrong, as they say, whereby it cometh to pass that one can scarcely know who is a noble woman, who is an honorable or worshipful Woman, from them of the meaner sort.

Stubbes might seem to wildly overstate the problem, but many contemporary observers agreed with him that Elizabethan people, especially those living in London, spent far too much money on clothes and were far too obsessed with outward appearance. ("I see that the fashion wears out more apparel than the man," says Conrade in *Much Ado About Nothing* [3.3.139–40].) Even the government was concerned, since much of the fine clothing being worn violated old ideas about the kinds of dress that were proper for different social classes. "Sumptuary laws," specifying exactly how people of different ranks and occupations should and should not dress, had long existed in England, but they were difficult to enforce and were constantly being broken. In 1574 the government issued another statute about attire; its phrasing is similar in many ways to the language used by Stubbes, and its list of prohibitions gives a vivid sense of the ways in which many men of all ranks and classes were dressing (and were supposed to dress) during Shakespeare's day, particularly in the capital.

The statute forbade any men except members of the royal family and other high-ranking people to wear any "silk of the color of purple, cloth of gold tissued, [or] fur of sables" and also "Cloth of gold, silver, tinseled satin, silk, or cloth mixed or embroidered with any gold or silver." Only aristocrats or prominent court officials could wear "Woolen cloth made out of the realm, but in caps only; velvet, crimson, or scarlet; furs, black [fur of] genets, lucerns [lynx furs]; embroidery or tailor's work having gold or silver or pearl therein." Only men of rank were permitted to wear "Velvet in gowns, coats, or other uttermost garments; fur of leopards; [or] embroidery with any silk," and the same was true of "Caps, hats, hatbands, capbands, garters, or boothose trimmed with gold or silver or pearl; silk netherstock[ing]s; enameled chains, buttons, [and] aglets." Likewise, only people who spent at least £100 per year (that is, wealthy people) were permitted to wear "Satin, damask, silk, camlet, or taffeta in gown, coat, hose, or uppermost garments" or "fur whereof the kind groweth not in the Queen's dominions, except foins [weasels], grey genets, and budge [a kind of lamb skin]." Only those of the rank of knight and above were supposed to wear "Hat, bonnet, girdle, scabbards of swords, daggers, etc.; [and] shoes and pantofles [slippers or loose shoes] of velvet," while only men of substantial incomes were supposed to wear "Silk other than satin, damask, taffeta, camlet, in doublets; and sarcanet, camlet, or taffeta in facing of gowns and cloaks, and in coats, jackets, jerkins, coifs, purses being not of the color scarlet, crimson, or blue; fur of foins, grey genets, or other as the like groweth not in the Queen's dominions." The statute also specified that "None shall wear spurs, swords, rapiers, daggers, skeans, woodknives, or hangers, buckles or girdles, gilt, silvered or damasked: except knights and barons' sons, and others of higher degree or place, and gentlemen in ordinary office attendant upon the Queen's majesty's person," just as people were not entitled to "wear in their trappings or harness of their horse any studs, buckles, or other garniture gilt, silvered, or damasked; nor stirrups gilt, silvered,

Portrait of Robert Dudley, a favorite of Queen Elizabeth I, ca. 1560s. The color, style, and material of Dudley's clothing indicate his high position in Elizabethan society. *(Attributed to Steven van Herqijck)*

or damasked; nor any velvet in saddles or horse trappers: except the persons next before mentioned and others of higher degree, and gentlemen in ordinary."

The statute goes on, in great detail, specifying the kinds of dress appropriate for women as well as men, but the sentences just quoted will give some sense of how extremely important dress could be to the Elizabethans, and of just how lavish the dress of many people was becoming. Not everyone could afford to buy sumptuous clothing: Apprentices typically wore simple blue coats and woolen caps. Nevertheless, numerous people in the bottom half of the social scale apparently purchased fine clothing that had been discarded by their betters as outdated or out of fashion. Few were the Elizabethans who could say, with Bianca in *The Taming of the Shrew*, "Old fashions please me best" (3.1.80). In fact, Fynes Moryson reported that when people of the lower ranks began wearing the clothing of their betters, it all the more quickly went out of fashion:

All manners of attire came first into the city and country from the court, which, being once received by the common people, and by the very stage-players themselves, the courtiers justly cast [it] off, and take new fashions. . . . For it is proverbially said, that we may eat according to our own appetite, but in our apparel must follow the fashion of the multitude, with whom we live.

Imagine London as a city full of people dressed in diverse ways while also being highly conscious of their own and of other people's dress, with nearly all people at all levels of the social hierarchy making some statement, merely through their clothing, about their social status and social aspirations.

AWAY FROM ST. PAUL'S: DOWN CHEAPSIDE STREET

However they dressed, most of the regular residents of London would have spent much of their time working at their various jobs, but what would a newcomer to the city—say, from Stratford-upon-Avon—have seen and done? A visit to St. Paul's Cathedral would have been high on the list of priorities, but after the visitor had strolled up and down the main aisle there a few times, seeing and being seen, what might be next on the agenda? Coming out of the cathedral into the churchyard, which was surrounded by houses and shops, a visitor would have noticed signs advertising stores owned by various stationers—that is, printers and booksellers. Henry Wheatley, in his invaluable three-volume account of *London Past and Present*, reports that

> At the sign of the White Greyhound, . . . the first editions of
> Shakespeare's *Venus and Adonis* and *Rape of Lucrece* were published by
> John Harrison; at the Flower de Luce and the Crown appeared the first
> edition of the *Merry Wives of Windsor*; at the Green Dragon the first
> edition of the *Merchant of Venice*; at the Fox the first edition of *Richard
> II*; at the Angel the first edition of *Richard III*; at the Spread Eagle the
> first edition of *Troilus and Cressida*; at the Gun the first edition of *Titus
> Andronicus*; and at the Red Bull the first edition of *Lear*.

Colorful, distinctive signs of these sorts were the common method of advertising in Elizabethan London; a shop was known not by a numerical address but by the name of its street and the nature of its sign.

Echoing the great London historian John Stow, Wheatley notes that on the north side of the churchyard stood "a pulpit Cross of timber, mounted

Illustration of Old St. Paul's Cathedral from Francis Bond's *An Introduction to English Church Architecture from the Eleventh to the Sixteenth Century*, volume 2, published in 1913.

upon steps of stone and covered with a conical roof of lead, from which sermons were preached by learned divines every Sunday in the forenoon." The sermons preached here were famous for their intellectual quality. Only the best preachers were invited to speak, and the audience included a wide cross section of London citizens, from the very least to the most important. The sermons were notoriously well attended, and finding seating was often difficult, even though services often lasted, according to Baron Waldstein, "for nearly three hours." Preachers of these outdoor sermons were expected to tow the government's line, although this did not happen as invariably as the government wished. Even so, sermons preached at Paul's were often printed and distributed throughout the rest of the country, where they were often preached once again in numerous local pulpits.

Near the cross, on the eastern side of the churchyard, was St. Paul's School, which was founded around 1509 to 1510 to educate poor children. Wheatley notes that originally the "boys were to be admitted without restriction of kin, country, or station" and were "to be taught, free of expense, by a master, sur-master, and chaplain." Like most English schoolboys, they were expected to learn Latin and Greek thoroughly, especially as those languages had been written by the best ancient authors. Yet these boys could also be rambunctious and were allowed—sometimes even encouraged—to participate in sports, depending on the attitude of the headmaster at any given time. Sometimes the boys sang, made speeches, or acted in plays, including before the queen herself. Boys who misbehaved too badly might be flogged, but the chance to be educated at St. Paul's was a great opportunity, and graduates often had successful and prominent careers.

Leaving the precincts of the cathedral and heading east, one walked along the broad, straight street known as Cheapside (mentioned twice in Shakespeare's *2 Henry VI*), which was the main east–west thoroughfare through the city. Paul Hentzner in 1598 was impressed in general with the streets of London, which he called "very handsome and clean," but he reported that Cheapside "surpasses all the rest." He noted that "there is in it a gilt tower, with a fountain" displaying splashing water, and "There are besides to be seen in this street, as in all others where there are goldsmiths' shops, all sorts of gold and silver vessels exposed to sale; as well as ancient and modern medals, in such quantities as must surprise a man the first time he sees and considers them." Cheapside—both the street and the neighborhood adjacent to it—was the commercial heart of the city. Foreign visitors were inevitably impressed, and residents of London themselves often commented on this street. Thus Isabella Whitney, in her poem about London published in 1573, described it as a place populated by goldsmiths who sold jewels for ladies, but she also commented that gold plate and silver were on sale there, along with various kinds of headgear, such as hoods, sunshades, hats, and caps. Ben Jonson depicted the street as a place where Londoners could be seen strolling in their plumes as they bought cherries and apricots, and in general one senses from contemporary accounts that Cheapside was a place of bustling commercial and social activity. Stephen Porter quotes the comments of Thomas Platter, who reported that "In one very long street called Cheapside dwell almost only goldsmiths and money changers on either hand, so that inexpressibly great treasures and vast amounts of money may be seen here," and Porter also quotes a German visitor who described Cheapside as "the finest and richest" street in London.

Cheapside, like many of the streets of London, was lined with shops of various kinds, most of them advertising themselves with signs projecting outward from the walls into the street itself. Above the shops were often the residences of the families who owned and ran the businesses. The buildings housing the shops and apartments were often built to a height of three or four stories, with each higher story slightly longer than the one below it, so that in the narrower streets (which were quite numerous) the tops of the buildings almost touched. Most of the commercial and residential buildings of London were built of timber and plaster, and many had thatched roofs made of straw, although tile roofs were increasingly common. Fires in such an environment could be enormously destructive—as London discovered especially in 1666, when most of the city burned to the ground. Extinguishing fires was extremely difficult, mainly because of a lack of ready or abundant supplies of water, which had to be carried to fires in leather buckets. Fires, as Porter notes, were often fought using long grappling hooks, which were used to pull down burning roofs or sometimes even entire buildings. Fire destroyed the original Globe Theatre, in which so many of Shakespeare's plays were first performed.

As a visitor walked eastward from St. Paul's down the broad thoroughfare of Cheapside Street, the church of St. Matthew Friday Street would be to the north, or left. Friday Street got its name, according to Stow, from the many "fish-mongers dwelling there, and serving Friday's market." The English were expected to eat fish on Fridays, and this street in London had been catering to that need since at least the Middle Ages. In this street was the famous "White Horse" tavern, where poet George Peele is supposed to have devised a trick to feed a poor, badly dressed friend. According to the story, Peele arranged for his friend to approach him while he was eating at the tavern with some fashionable companions and to pretend to be an insulting stranger. Peele then supposedly pretended to be so outraged by the stranger's comments that he threw food at him, including two rabbits and some bread, so his upscale dining partners never suspected the ruse.

Walking farther east along Cheapside, one came to Edward I's "Great Cross," which stood in the middle of the wide street, having been erected there in 1290. An imposing, stately structure made of stone, this monument was often gilded to give it the appearance of glimmering gold. When Shakespeare lived in London, the large wooden cross at the top of the monument had fallen into disrepair and was even considered a public hazard, and some radical Protestants even found it religiously offensive. Eventually, a new cross was installed by the order of the queen and her top courtiers and was covered with gilded lead. Anyone walking down Cheapside away from St. Paul's could not have missed being struck—some feared literally—by this huge structure.

Further along Cheapside, again heading east, one encountered Goldsmith's Row, which was on the right (or southern) end of the street. Stow called this row "the most beautiful frame of fair houses and shops that be within the walls of London, or elsewhere in England. . . . It containeth in number ten fair dwelling-houses and fourteen shops, all in one frame, uniformly built four storeys high, beautified towards the street with the Goldsmiths' [coat of] Arms and the likeness of Woodmen . . . riding on monstrous beasts, all which is cast in lead, richly painted over and gilt." At the eastern end of Goldsmith's Row, standing right in the middle of Cheapside, was a huge stone water conduit—the one that had so impressed Hentzner—called "the Standard in Cheap." Clean water, always a valuable commodity in London, flowed into the city from the suburbs through lead pipes and emerged at the Standard, but the conduit had also traditionally been a place where public proclamations were made and where public punishments were carried out.

At the eastern end of Goldsmith's Row was Bread Street, on the right (or southern) side of Cheapside as one moved away from St. Paul's. Bread Street had traditionally been the center of London's baking industry, but Stow noted in 1603 that it "is now wholly inhabited by rich merchants; and diverse fair inns be there, for good receipt of carriers and other travelers to the city." Three of these inns were named "The Star," "The Three Cups," and "The George," and any travelers who stayed there had certainly chosen convenient lodgings close to the center of the city. The great poet John Milton was born in Bread Street in 1608, while Shakespeare was still living, and Milton's father worked as a scrivener (a professional copyist or scribe) in a shop bearing the sign of "The Spread Eagle." A prison had once existed in this street, but it had been moved to a new location in 1555.

Past Bread Street, farther east on the right (or south) side of Cheapside, lay the lofty church of St. Mary-le-Bow, with its tall stone bell tower. Stow called it a "fair parish church" and noted that it had been "the first in this city built of arches of stone," back in the eleventh century. Because of its storied history, Stow considered it "more famous than any other parish church in the whole city or suburbs." Its bells were especially well known, as was an imposing stone structure just to the north of the churchyard, facing Cheapside, called the "Crown Sild" gallery, where English monarchs, foreign dignitaries, and other important figures often gathered to behold, from the second story, "the shows of this city passing through West Cheap, namely, the great watches accustomed in the night, on the even of St. John the Baptist, and St. Peter at Midsummer." According to Stow, King Henry VIII in 1510 supposedly came to this gallery "in the livery of a yeoman of the guard, with a halbert on his shoulder, and there beholding the watch, departed privily when the watch was done, and was not known to any but whom it pleased him."

Several blocks farther past the "Crown Sild" was Mercer's Hall, the massive gathering place of one of the most prominent of the livery companies. Almost directly in front of the hall, in the middle of the street, was the Great Conduit. It had existed since the thirteenth century, bringing fresh, clean water into the heart of the city from a stream outside of town. A smaller conduit, with a weaker stream and therefore known as the "Pissing Conduit," was a bit farther east. This smaller conduit was quite close to the Stocks Market, so-called, according to Stow, because at one time in the distant past it was the site of "a pair of stocks for the punishment of offenders." In Stow's day the market sold "fish and flesh," with scores of separate stalls operated by bustling butchers and fishmongers. Finally, slightly farther east of the Stocks Market lay the impressive new Royal Exchange, a huge, square, open-air mall that had been officially opened by the queen in 1571. It was designed, Stow said, as "a place for merchants to assemble," and at the royal opening trumpets were sounded as the queen inspected the various shops "richly furnished with all sorts of the finest wares in the city."

SITE-SEEING AND SIGHT-SEEING

Having arrived at the Royal Exchange and perhaps having spent some time shopping, a visitor might next stop by the famous "hospital of St. Mary of Bethlehem," which was not far beyond the city's northern walls and was right next to a major inn, whose guests often visited the hospital, according to Stow. "Bedlam," as it was commonly called, had been founded in the thirteenth century and had become notorious as a "hospital for distracted people" (that is, for the insane). Stow noted that "In this place people that be distraught in wits are, by the suit of their friends, received and kept, . . . but not without charges to their bringers in." Treatment of the more seriously afflicted inmates amounted to little more than restraint with ropes and chains, and the screams emanating from inside the buildings could be horrendous. Yet Wheatley notes that by "the beginning of the 17th century Bethlehem Hospital had become one of the London sights, and so it continued until the last quarter of the 18th century." Various evidence suggests that the tamer inmates were sometimes sent out into the streets to beg, where they were regarded as one of the sights of London. Meanwhile, visitors could also pay fees to be admitted to view the inmates who remained confined inside. Even official inspectors in 1598 found conditions at the hospital filthy and appalling; little wonder that "bedlam" had already become by Shakespeare's day a synonym for madness, poverty, disorder, and chaos. Shakespeare, of course, makes much of these associations in *King Lear*, where Edgar speaks of "Bedlam beggars, who, with roaring voices, / Strike in their numb'd and mortified bare arms / Pins, wooden pricks, nails, [and] sprigs of rosemary" (2.3.1265–67).

If "Bedlam" sounds more like a prison than a hospital, there were also plenty of proper jails and prisons in the city. John Taylor, the minor poet, counted 18 of them during Shakespeare's era, including such places as Bridewell, The Clink, East Smithfield Prison, Fleet Prison, The King's Bench, The Hole at St. Katherines, Ludgate, The Marshalsea, Newgate, New Prison, The White Lion, and various scattered "Counters" (city prisons or jails). Pris-

Seventeenth-century woodcut of Newgate Prison in London. Outside the prison, two people have been hanged. Meanwhile, two prisoners appear to be trying to escape.

oners could be committed for numerous offences, from debt and minor trespasses to serious crimes such as murder, and visitors were frequently allowed. Conditions were often extremely unappealing (little wonder, then, that the ghost of Hamlet's father compares the horrors of purgatory to those of a "prison-house" [1.5.14]). Far worse, however, were what William Harrison referred to, in the title of one of his chapters, as the "Sundry Kinds of Punishments Appointed to Malefactors." Many of these punishments would have been carried out in public places in London; they were meant to be witnessed and to deter others from similar crimes. Harrison noted that hanging was common in "cases of felony, manslaughter, robbery, murder, rape, piracy, and such capital crimes as are not reputed for treason or hurt of the estate." The last of these crimes were so serious that prisoners were supposed to be drawn "from the prison to the place of execution upon an hurdle or sled, where they are hanged till they be half dead, and then taken down, and quartered alive; after that, their members and bowels are cut from their bodies, and thrown into a fire, provided near hand and within their own sight, even for the same purpose."

Members of the aristocracy were cut a certain slack: They were often beheaded rather than hanged. (As Claudius comments ironically in *Hamlet*, "Where th' offense is, let the great axe fall" [4.5.219].) But a common person "convicted of willful murder, done either upon pretended malice or in any notable robbery," was "either hanged alive in chains near the place where the fact was committed (or else upon compassion taken, first strangled with a rope), and so continueth till his bones consume to nothing." Harrison reported that "when willful manslaughter [was] perpetrated, beside hanging, the offender hath his right hand commonly stricken off before or near unto the place where the act was done, after which he is led forth to the place of execution, and there put to death according to the law."

"Rogues and vagabonds," Harrison noted, were

> often stocked and whipped; scolds are ducked upon cucking-stools in the water. Such felons as stand mute, and speak not at their arraignment, are pressed to death by huge weights laid upon a board, that lieth over their breast, and a sharp stone under their backs; and these commonly hold their peace, thereby to save their goods unto their wives and children, which, if they were condemned, should be confiscated to the prince. . . . Pirates and robbers by sea are condemned in the Court of the Admiralty, and hanged on the shore

at low-water mark, where they are left till three tides have overwashed them.

Public punishments of criminals would have been a fairly common sight in London and would have added to the excitement of living in (or merely visiting) the metropolis. Many Elizabethans would have agreed with Clifford in *3 Henry VI* when he asks rhetorically, "what makes robbers bold but too much lenity?" (2.6.22). Severe punishments were intended to teach memorable lessons, although there always seemed to be more criminals in need of such instruction.

LECTURES AND LEARNING

Anyone interested in education of a less morbid sort could attend various public lectures. Stow notes, for instance, that beginning in 1584 a series of lectures on medicine had been established. These lectures were "to be read in the College of Physicians" and were "to be continued for ever, twice every week, on Wednesday and Friday." Likewise, a series of mathematical lectures was also endowed, although the location of these talks altered over time. Most famously, perhaps, Sir Thomas Gresham—the wealthy businessman who had been the leading mover behind the establishment of the Royal Exchange—also endowed a series of lectures to be given in his own impressive home after he and his widow died. Qualified lecturers were to be found to speak on topics such as divinity, astronomy, music, geometry, civil law, "physic," and rhetoric. The lectures began in 1597 and were supposed "to continue for ever."

London was also home to a number of impressive schools for boys. (Most intelligent Elizabethans would have recognized the humor when Jack Cade accuses Lord Saye in *2 Henry VI* of having "most traitorously corrupted the youth of the realm [by] erecting a grammar school" [4.7.32–34].) St. Paul's School, near the cathedral, has been mentioned, but another of these establishments was the Merchant Taylors School, much closer to the river and to London Bridge. It was established in 1561. Its first and perhaps most famous headmaster was Richard Mulcaster, the noted educational theorist who stressed the acquisition not only of Latin but also Greek and Hebrew and who was especially concerned that children should master the English language in a clear series of logically organized steps. Like the boys at St. Paul's School, where Mulcaster would later serve briefly as headmaster, those affiliated with the Merchant Taylors School learned music and put on plays (often before the monarch), and they also competed in sports. Perhaps the most interesting account of competition among young students of this period was left by Stow, who reports that, although some kinds of academic disputations had long since been discontinued,

> the arguing of the schoolboys about the principles of grammar hath been continued even till our time; for I myself, in my youth, have yearly seen, on the eve of St Bartholomew the Apostle, the scholars of divers grammar-schools repair unto the churchyard of St Bartholomew, the priory in Smithfield, where upon a bank boarded about under a tree, some one scholar hath stepped up, and there both

MEDICINE

Medicine in Shakespeare's era was rudimentary by modern standards, but trained and licensed physicians were increasingly common, and barber-surgeons were also on the rise. Folk remedies were still widely employed, but genuine empirical discoveries, such as William Harvey's discovery of the circulation of blood, were either being made or were on the horizon during Shakespeare's lifetime. In general, this was a period in which medicine began to make some real scientific progress, partly because of the increasingly common study of the human anatomy through the dissection of corpses. English physicians often studied abroad and brought home the latest continental discoveries, and the rise of the printing press meant that scientific knowledge of all kinds could be more easily and quickly shared throughout Europe. Foreign physicians sometimes came to Protestant England to avoid religious persecution in their own countries, and so medical knowledge began to circulate more widely than had been the case a century earlier.

Drugs and other forms of medicine were often derived from plants, and doctors were often gardeners with expertise in botany, particularly in herbs. Surgery—from tooth extractions to amputations—was brutal and extremely painful by modern standards. Alcohol was the most common form of anesthetic. Other drugs were either homemade or were purchased from "apothecaries," who were sometimes accused of charging excessive prices. Secret remedies were sometimes employed both by respectable physicians and by obvious quacks, but pain was widespread in Shakespeare's day.

"By med'cine life may be prolong'd, yet death
Will seize the doctor too."
— *Cymbeline* (5.5.29–30)

opposed and answered till he were by some better scholar overcome and put down; and then the overcomer taking the place, did like as the first; and in the end the best opposers and answerers had rewards, which I observed not but it made both good schoolmasters and also good scholars, diligently against such times to prepare themselves for the obtaining of this garland.

Perhaps the most important of all the educational establishments in London were the so-called "Inns of Court," which consisted of four main residential halls (in addition to 10 lesser ones known as the Inns of Chancery) intended to provide housing, headquarters, and training for the city's lawyers, of whom there were ever-growing numbers. By the beginning of the sixteenth century the four great Inns of Court—Gray's, Lincoln's, Inner Temple, and Middle Temple—had won a wide reputation as centers of legal education, and Sir Edward Coke, the famous lawyer and legal scholar, could even call the combined Inns of Court and Chancery (with some exaggeration) "the most famous university for the profession of law only, or of any humane science, that is in the world." Stow agreed that the Inns constituted almost a group of colleges, saying that "there is in and about this city a whole university, as it were, of students, practicers or pleaders, and judges of the laws of this realm, not living of common stipends as of other universities it is for the most part done, but of their own private maintenance, as being altogether fed either by their places or practice, or otherwise by their proper revenue, or exhibition of parents or friends; for that the younger sort are either gentlemen, or sons of gentlemen, or of other most wealthy persons." Law was a lucrative profession in Shakespeare's day, but lawyers were often widely distrusted. Both facts help explain the rebel Dick the Butcher's famous comment in *2 Henry VI* as he contemplates an uprising: "The first thing we do, let's kill all the lawyers" (4.2.76–77).

Students often lived at the Inns for seven years, mastering the law and practicing the arguing of cases. They thereby rose in rank within their own societies and won the right to practice in the courts of common law. By one estimate, the four main Inns probably housed about a thousand people by 1600, many of whom were less interested in becoming lawyers than in acquiring the cultural polish and social connections that came from living among other bright, ambitious, and literate young men. For many of these people the main attraction of living in London was not so much the chance to practice as lawyers in courts of law but rather the opportunity to angle for position and preferment in the most

An 1895 illustration of Middle Temple Hall. *(Herbert Railton)*

important court of all: the royal court of the queen or king. London, after all, was not merely the center of English law and commerce. It was the headquarters—for most of the year, at least—of the English monarch.

Sources and Further Reading

Besant, Walter. *London in the Time of the Tudors*. London: Adam and Charles Black, 1904. Print.

Chalfant, Fran C. *Ben Jonson's London: A Jacobean Placename Dictionary*. Athens: University of Georgia Press, 1978. Print.

Compton-Rickett, Arthur. *The London Life of Yesterday*. London: Constable, 1909. Print.

Picard, Liza. *Elizabeth's London: Everyday Life in Elizabethan London*. New York: St. Martin's Griffin, 2003. Print.

Porter, Stephen. *Shakespeare's London: Everyday Life in London 1580–1616*. Chalford, Gloucestershire: Amberley, 2009. Print.

Stow, John. *A Survey of London*. Ed. Charles Lethbridge Kingsford. 2 vols. Oxford: Clarendon, 1971. Print.

Wheatley, Henry. *London, Past and Present: Its History, Associations, and Traditions*. 3 vols. London: J. Murray, 1891. Print.

DAILY LIFE AT COURT

The royal "court" during Shakespeare's time was not so much a definite physical place as it was an amorphous zone or sphere of influence. Wherever the monarch happened to be, there also was the court. Although Queen Elizabeth I and King James VI and I— King James VI of Scotland became King James I of England after Elizabeth's death when Scotland was united with England—spent much of their time dwelling in residences in or near London, "the court" moved with them whenever and wherever they moved, and both of these monarchs liked to move often. They regularly shuttled from one palace to another, and often they (especially Elizabeth) went on elaborate yearly "progresses," journeying across the land with numerous courtiers and many heavily laden carts in tow. They stopped and stayed for days at a time at royal residences and private houses along the way, thereby essentially taking the court to distant towns and into the distant countryside.

For much of the year, however, the monarch was in or near London—especially in the neighboring city of Westminster, the site of Whitehall, a key royal palace, and also of much of the permanent infrastructure of the English government, particularly the most important courts of law. Many of the most significant structures associated with royal power—including the imposing Tower of London—were either in the capital or not far away. In the truest sense, though, the royal court consisted not so much of permanent physical buildings but of intangible, constantly shifting and unstable relationships. The most important of these relationships—especially for those near the top of the social pyramid—was always with the monarch. Yet the monarch's own mind and feelings could change from day to day or moment to moment. A courtier who enjoyed enormous power and influence one day might easily lose it (or much of it) the next. Likewise, those whose own status in society depended greatly on their relations with that particular courtier could win or lose according to their patron's profits or losses.

The court was a site of enormous ambition and constant competition and self-display, but it was also a site of inevitable instability. No one's position was really safe or secure—not even the monarch's. The court was invariably described as a kind of slippery slope where it was always easy to lose one's balance. Thus Belarius in *Cymbeline* says that "the art o' th' court

[is] / As hard to leave as keep; whose top to climb / Is certain falling, or so slipp'ry that / The fear's as bad as falling" (3.3.46–49).

THE TOWER OF LONDON

A visitor to England in Shakespeare's day would have been less instantly aware of the internal dynamics of life at court than of the external manifestations of royal power and magnificence, especially the buildings owned or controlled by the monarch. In London, the most impressive of these was the ancient Tower of London, which stood south and west of Cheapside, not far from London Bridge. Work on this imposing stone structure had begun in the late eleventh century, by William the Conqueror, and successive monarchs had added to the complex of buildings in the centuries that followed. Thus, by Shakespeare's time the Tower consisted most obviously of a tall, sturdy fortress surrounded by thick stone walls enclosing various outlying structures. Once a royal residence, the Tower had now chiefly become, in John A. Wagner's words, "the royal mint, armory, and zoo, but it was used mainly as a state prison and the site of state executions." Various members

Tower of London. *(Photograph by Aaron Headly)*

of the royal family, including Queen Elizabeth before she became queen, had been imprisoned there, and some had even died or been executed there, including Elizabeth's mother. Visitors to London were always impressed by the Tower—and they still are: It had been built to seem intimidating, and so it was and remains to this day. Thus Paul Hentzner, the German who toured London in 1598, described it as follows:

> The Castle, or Tower of London, called Bringwin, and Tourgwin, in Welsh, from its whiteness, is encompassed by a very deep and broad ditch, as well as a double wall very high. In the middle of the whole is that very ancient and very strong tower, enclosed with four others. . . . Upon entering the tower, we were obliged to quit our swords at the gate, and deliver them to the guard. When we were introduced, we were shown above a hundred pieces of arras belonging to the crown, made of gold, silver, and silk; several saddles covered with velvet of different colors; an immense quantity of bed-furniture, such as canopies, and the like, some of them most richly ornamented with pearl; some royal dresses, so extremely magnificent, as to raise any one's admiration at the sums they must have cost. We were next led into the armory, in which are these particularities: spears, out of which you may shoot; shields, that will give fire four times; a great many rich halberds, commonly called partuisans, with which the guard defend the royal person in battle; some lances, covered with red and green velvet, and the body-armor of Henry VIII; many, and very beautiful arms, as well for men, as for horses in horse-fights; the lance of Charles Brandon duke of Suffolk, three spans thick; two pieces of cannon, the one fires three, the other seven balls at a time; two others made of wood; . . . nineteen cannon, of a thicker make than ordinary; and in a room apart; thirty-six of a smaller; other cannon for chain-shot; and balls proper to bring down masts of ships. Cross-bows, bows and arrows, of which to this day the English make great use in their exercises: but who can relate all that is to be seen here? Eight or nine men, employed by the year, are scarce sufficient to keep all the arms bright.

Not only the arms housed in the Tower, however, impressed Hentzner; so did the animals:

> On coming out of the tower, we were led to a small house close by, where are kept a variety of creatures, viz. three lionesses, one lion of

great size, called Edward VI, from his having been born in that reign; a tiger; a lynx; a wolf excessively old; . . . there is besides, a porcupine, and an eagle. All these creatures are kept in a remote place, fitted up for the purpose with wooden lattices at the queen's expense.

The zoo at the Tower attracted not only foreign visitors but also the British themselves, including the monarchs. Several accounts from the time of

EXPLORATION OF THE NEW WORLD

The sixteenth century was the first major period of European colonialism in the so-called "New World" of North and South America. In particular, Spain and Portugal —two of Protestant England's greatest Catholic enemies—had begun to develop vast empires in the new territories, and Spain reaped lucrative rewards (especially in the mining of gold) from its new overseas possessions. The English were latecomers to American colonialism, although by Shakespeare's day there was increasing interest both in establishing English colonies and in profiting (through privateering) from the colonies already established by Spain. Sir Francis Drake (ca. 1543–1596) was perhaps the most famous and successful of the Elizabethan privateers. Nicknamed "the Dragon" by the Spanish, Drake—with the quiet support of the English government—plundered Spanish ships on the high seas, bringing his loot back to England to share with the many people (including Queen Elizabeth) who had helped finance his expeditions. On one of these trips (lasting from 1577 to 1580), Drake sailed around the world, adding to his own reputation as an explorer and to England's reputation as one of the most adventurous of seafaring nations.

Other English explorers, privateers, and colonialists included such men as John Hawkins, Martin Frobisher, John Davis, and Sir Walter Raleigh, the last of whom tried unsuccessfully to establish an English colony in North America in modern-day Virginia (named after the Virgin Queen). Before long, the English succeeded in their efforts to colonize parts of America, especially what is now the United States and Canada. By the beginning of Shakespeare's career, America had attracted the attention of numerous people in England. "Indians" from America were sometimes brought back to England, along with numerous products (such as tobacco). In the decades following Shakespeare's death, numerous English people would set off for America, partly in pursuit of a kind of religious liberty they could not enjoy at home.

"One inch of delay more is a South Sea of discovery."
— *As You Like It* (3.2.196–97)

King James report how that ruler staged vicious fights between the lion and various intrepid dogs (with the lion the inevitable, if often badly wounded, victor), and once a lamb was even lowered into the lion's den and, to the surprise of everyone, showed little fright and was basically ignored by the king of beasts.

UP THE THAMES, TOWARD WESTMINSTER

Hentzner noted that not far from the Tower (but across the Thames, near the theaters in Southwark) lay "the royal barge, close to the river; it has two splendid cabins, beautifully ornamented with glass windows, painting and gilding; it is kept upon dry ground, and sheltered from the weather." Farther up the banks of the river, on the northern side and heading east, lay various wharves (sometimes called "keys") as well as an especially imposing building known as Baynard's Castle—an ancient structure that had recently been a royal palace but was owned, during Shakespeare's era, by the aristocratic Pembroke family. A few blocks to the west of this castle lay Bridewell, formerly a royal palace but during Shakespeare's time a workhouse and prison. Next came Whitefriars, site of a former residence for monks but now occupied by impressive private homes and the location, beginning in 1606, of a private theater in the former refectory hall of the ancient monastery.

Farther west along the river lay the Inner Temple (one of the Inns of Court), then the Middle Temple (another legal Inn), and then Arundel House, briefly a royal possession but, by Shakespeare's day, the London home of the earls of Arundel. Next came Somerset House (a royal residence at this time), then the Savoy. This was a former palace that had been turned into a hospital, although by Elizabethan times it had acquired an unsavory reputation as a hangout for rogues and other undisciplined people.

Immediately to the west was Bedford House, the London townhouse of the earls of Bedford, then Durham House, for a while the residence of Sir Walter Raleigh,

Illustration of Sir Walter Raleigh from the 1904 edition of Montgomery's *The Beginner's American History*.

the famous courtier. Near this (and back from the river) was a market known as the New Exchange, and then slightly to the west along the banks of the river was York House, which during Shakespeare's era was the London residence of the Lord Keepers of the Great Seal, among the most important officials in the royal court. As the river began to curve sharply to the south, Hungerford House appeared next on the northwestern bank, then Scotland Yard, once a residence for monarchs and ambassadors from Scotland. By this time a traveler had officially moved from the city of London to the adjacent city of Westminster, home of the chief royal palace of Whitehall. The main stairs from the Thames to the palace were just beyond Scotland Yard, followed by the Privy Stairs, used by the monarch and the royal courtiers to enter and exit barges on the river. Carefully designed gardens were close by, and next to these was Whitehall Palace itself. This was the main seat of royal government, although Shakespeare mentions it only once explicitly and only in passing (*Henry VIII* [4.1.97]).

WESTMINSTER AND WESTMINSTER HALL

To enter the palace on the ground, from Westminster, one had to pass through two large gates: Whitehall Gate and King Street Gate. Along the river, and within the palace complex, was a group of buildings called Canon Row, which provided lodgings for courtiers and aristocrats. Then came a major entrance into the grounds from the Thames known as Westminster Stairs. Next came the infamous and dreaded Court of Star Chamber, headquarters of a special court made up of top officials who could impose extraordinary punishments on people suspected by the government of serious (or even minor) criminal conduct. (This court is mentioned only once, in passing, by Shakespeare, in *The Merry Wives of Windsor* [1.1.2].) To the west and south of this was Westminster Hall. This, as Stephen Porter notes in his excellent book on Tudor and Stuart London, was

> the location for the courts of common law and equity from the
> late twelfth century and for King's Bench from the early fifteenth
> century. By the late Middle Ages three courts met in Westminster
> Hall: Chancery and King's Bench on either side of the south end,
> and Common Pleas along the west wall. The three equity courts
> of Chancery, Exchequer and Requests had grown up alongside the
> common law courts and . . . heard cases where those without 'remedy
> in the common law' could seek redress 'according to equity and

reason'. All of them attracted much business from a wide social range. Requests and Exchequer had developed in the sixteenth century, Requests as a court accessible to 'poor men'.

It was partly to conduct legal business in these courts that so many people from throughout England visited London and Westminster in Shakespeare's era, and Westminster Hall was notoriously noisy because it was filled with lawyers and their clients and vendors of various kinds. The hall was also the traditional assembly place of English Parliaments. These did not meet constantly, as the U.S. Congress now does, but instead sat only when summoned by the monarch. (Thus Prince John, in *2 Henry IV*, mentions that "The king hath called his parliament, my lord" [5.5.103].) During sessions of Parliament, Westminster Hall was even more a place for people (in this case, quite important people) from throughout the land to congregate. During his 1598 visit to England, Paul Hentzner noted that in "the chamber where the parliament is usually held, the seats and wainscot are made of wood, the growth of Ireland; said to have that occult quality, that all poisonous animals are driven away by it."

QUEEN ELIZABETH OPENS PARLIAMENT

An especially detailed description of the opening of Parliament survives from a diary by a German tourist, Leopold von Wedel, who visited England from 1584 to 1585 and left an account of the sumptuous and highly ceremonial opening of Parliament in November 1584:

> All the streets and lanes in Westminster were well cleaned and strewn
> with sand when the queen made her entrance into the house. . . .
> At the head of the procession rode, two by two, eighteen lords and
> gentlemen of the court, after them fifteen trumpets, two gentlemen,
> each with 100 soldiers uniformly clad; now came fifteen members
> of Parliament in long red cloth coats, lined with white rabbit and
> reverses of the same almost down to the girdle. Next followed two
> gentlemen, the first with the queen's mantle, the other with her hat,
> their horses were led by servants. Now came two heralds, each in a
> blue mantle with two wings on it of beaten gold bearing the queen's
> arms, then three pairs of gentlemen of the Parliament in their usual
> robes, two heralds like those before followed by thirteen gentlemen of
> the Parliament, counts and barons, like the former, two heralds, seven
> pairs of bishops in long red robes with broad reverses of white linen

and square caps of black stuff on their heads, then came five pairs of gentlemen of the Parliament in long red coats set with four stripes of rabbit fur. Now followed the Chancellor of the realm, behind him the Treasurer and the Secretary in their usual robes, with broad golden collars hanging down in the front and back to the saddle. Followed four men with sceptres, each ornamented with a crown, followed some gentlemen of the Parliament like the others. All these, I have mentioned, had gold and silver trappings on their horses, the least valuable being velvet. Followed the huntsmen, about fifty in number, all of noble birth, with small spears. These marched on foot. Now followed a horse, led by a gentleman, the trappings, saddle and bridle all of gold covered with pearls, the latter being set with precious stones. On the forehead an ornament was fixed with one large diamond, and on the ears hung pearls.

Von Wedel, whose account is little known and rarely reprinted and therefore seems worth quoting at length, was particularly impressed by the appearance of Elizabeth:

Now followed the queen in a half-covered sedan chair, which looked like a half-covered Bed. The chair and the cushions on which the queen was seated were covered with gold and silver cloth. The queen had a long red velvet parliamentary mantle, down to the waist, lined with ermine, white with little black dots, and a crown on her head.

One recalls the words of Cleopatra in Shakespeare's play: "Show me, my women, like a queen; go fetch / My best attires" (5.2.227–28). Von Wedel continues:

The sedan chair was carried by two cream-colored horses with yellow manes and tails, on the heads and tails yellow and white plumes were fastened, and they had saddles and trappings of golden stuff. Behind the queen another horse was led, having trappings of red velvet fringed with gold and ornamented with plumes. . . . On both sides of the queen marched her guard, not in their daily suit, but clad in red cloth, covered with beaten gold. The procession took its way to Westminster Church [present-day Westminster Abbey], where all the kings are buried. Here the queen dismounted, knelt down at the entrance and said her prayers, entered the church, where prayers were offered and chants performed.

Queen Elizabeth I presides over Parliament, ca. 1580–1600.

Inside as well as outside, the opening of what Henry V calls "our high court of parliament" (2 Henry IV [4.2.3382]) was an impressive sight:

> Then the queen went to the house of Parliament close by, and was led into a separate chamber, on the platform of which was a splendid canopy of golden stuff and velvet, embroidered with gold, silver and pearls, and below it a throne, arranged with royal splendors, on which the queen seated herself. The benches in this chamber had their seats as well as the backs covered with red silk, in the midst four woolsacks of red cloth were laid square. The walls were entirely hung with royal tapestry. In front of the woolsacks opposite the door a low bar was fixed right across the chamber, also covered with red silk. On the woolsack nearest to the queen's throne sits the Chancellor, turning his back to the queen, on that to the right hand sit three judges, on that to the left three secretaries. Close to the bar, but outside of it, sit two [writing] clerks, on the benches around to the right side twenty bishops, two viscounts or peers, one marquis, to the left twenty counts and twenty barons. Thus the sitting of this Parliament began, they had sittings every day until Christmas, but the queen, as I said before, was present only on the first and last day.

THE PALACE OF WHITEHALL: OUTSIDE

The palace complex at Westminster was used only intermittently for sessions of Parliament. Its more common function was to serve as the main royal residence and seat of royal government, and the palace of Whitehall was central to both of these purposes. Once again, von Wedel provides an especially valuable account, this time of his visit to Whitehall itself, where he and his companions

> first saw the tilt-yard [a place for jousting], besides a ball-house, where they play at featherballs [golf balls stuffed with feathers]. There is also a long-stretched building, in which they [bowl] with wooden balls. Upstairs the gentlemen play, the common people below. . . . This is called the 'Boule-house.' Hence we went into the queen's garden, in which there are thirty-four high columns, covered with various fine paintings; also different animals carved in wood, with their horns [of] gilt, are set on the top of the columns, together with flags bearing the queen's arms. In the middle of the garden is a nice fountain with a remarkable sun-dial, showing the time in thirty different ways.

Between the spices that are planted in the garden there are fine walks grown with grass, and the spices are planted very artistically, surrounded by plants in the shape of seats. Close to this garden there is an orchard; at the foot of the trees aromatic plants are planted.

The "tilt-yard" mentioned by von Wedel at Whitehall was the scene of one of the most important annual events in the Elizabethan calendar—the Accession Day tournament, held on November 17, the anniversary of Elizabeth's accession to the English throne. Von Wedel describes the tournament as follows:

About twelve o'clock the queen with her ladies placed themselves at the windows in a long room of *Weithol* (Whitehall) palace, near Westminster, opposite the barrier (lists) where the tournament was to be held. From this room a broad staircase led downwards, and round the barrier stands were arranged by boards above the ground, so that everybody by paying 12*d.* could get a stand and see the play. . . . Many thousand spectators, men, women and girls, got places, not to speak of those who were within the barrier and paid nothing. During the whole time of the tournament all who wished to fight entered the list by pairs, the trumpets being blown at the time and other musical instruments. The combatants had their servants clad in different colors, they, however, did not enter the barrier, but arranged themselves on both sides.

The tournaments were occasions for lavish spectacle:

Some of the servants were disguised like savages, or like Irishmen, with the hair hanging down to the girdle like women, others had horse manes on their heads, some came driving in a carriage, the horses being equipped like elephants, some carriages were drawn by men, others appeared to move by themselves; altogether the carriages were of very odd appearance. Some gentlemen had their horses with them and mounted in full armor directly from the carriage. There were some who showed very good horsemanship and were also in fine attire. . . . When a gentleman with his servant approached the barrier, on horseback or in a carriage, he stopped at the foot of the staircase leading to the queen's room, while one of his servants in pompous attire of a special pattern mounted the steps and addressed the queen in well-composed verses or with a ludicrous speech, making her and her ladies laugh.

In this, as in so many aspects of life at court, decorum ruled:

> When the speech was ended he in the name of his lord offered to the
> queen a costly present, which was accepted and permission given to
> take part in the tournament. In fact, however, they make sure of the
> permission before preparing for the combat. Now always two by two
> rode against each other, breaking lances across the beam. On this day
> not only many fine horses were seen, but also beautiful ladies, not
> only in the royal suite, but likewise in the company of gentlemen of
> the nobility and the citizens.

Obviously these tiltings made a vivid impression on the German visitors,
and they probably also impressed the many English people who also lined up
to watch them. Shakespeare's works contain a number of references to tiltings, as when Celia in *As You Like It* mockingly describes another character
as "a puisne [puny] tilter, that spurs his horse but on one side, [and] breaks
his staff like a noble goose" (3.4.43–45).

THE PALACE OF WHITEHALL: INSIDE

Von Wedel and his friends were able to visit not only the exterior grounds of
the palace but also its even more impressive interior:

> A man, in whose keeping the rooms of the palace are, took us out
> of the garden and led us to see the inner part of the palace, to which
> there are only two keys. On mounting a staircase we got into a
> passage right across the tiltyard; the ceiling is gilt, and the floor
> ornamented with mats. There were fine paintings on the walls, among
> them the portrait of Edward, the present queen's brother. . . . We were
> led into the queen's audience chamber, which is very large and high
> with gilt ceiling, upon which, on tablets, are written the dates of wars
> that have been made. The queen's bedroom has also a gilt ceiling, but
> only one window. In the room which the late king inhabited, whilst
> living, the Privy Council is now held. Here is a fine chimney-piece
> with the royal arms cut in a stone as clear as crystal, with two lions as
> supporters. We were taken into a long passage across the water, which
> on both sides is beautifully decorated with shields and mottoes. These
> shields originate from tournaments which the queen orders to be held
> twice a year, the first on her birthday, the second when she ascended
> the throne. Everybody who wishes to take part must ask permission;

this being granted, he offers the shield to the queen, who orders it to be hung up there.

In this passage the queen has secret doors to the river if she wishes to take a trip on the water. Then we were brought to a grass plot surrounded by broad walks below and above, enabling many persons to promenade there. In the middle of the place a pulpit is erected, with a sounding board above. When the queen commands preaching here, the walks are filled with auditors.

Both inside and outside, Whitehall was impressive:

Hence we were brought into a high and spacious house with many windows and inside full of seats and benches one above the other, so that many people may be seated there. The ceiling is hung with leaves and thick bushes. When foreign gentlemen are present, the queen orders all sorts of amusements to be arranged here, while above in the bushes birds sing beautifully. . . . In another room they showed us tapestry of silver cloth, on which were embroidered various animals in gold. This tapestry is fixed to the wall for the queen to lean against. Besides this was a red velvet cover, embroidered with gold, to be used when she goes in her barge, also long red velvet coats, lined and faced with costly white fur. The coats were embroidered with gold, and caps lined with the same fur, and long big tassels on the top. Such coats and caps are for the gentlemen of Parliament. . . . Almost in every room there was a musical instrument with silver-gilt ornaments and lined with velvet; one of these looked like a large high box, and contained in the interior various other instruments, and among these one that made music by itself. In short, the interior of the palace is very beautiful and royal indeed; the exterior did not differ from many other houses I have visited. I saw even several of a finer exterior, but the latter did not equal this on the inside. After having seen all this, we went to the royal stables, which are built square with a large court, in the middle of which is a fountain. A large number of horses can be kept here; we found the stables empty, the queen being absent. We saw another royal house [St. James's Palace] not very distant, with three courtyards, a garden, many large rooms, and a remarkable exterior; but the inside did not come up to the house before mentioned, also the queen does not often stay there.

Three times—in three different plays—Shakespeare uses the phrase "gorgeous palace," and perhaps he had Whitehall in mind when doing so.

INSIDE WHITEHALL: ANOTHER PERSPECTIVE

Many of the details von Wedel records about Whitehall were also visible when Paul Hentzner, another German, visited there 14 years later, in 1598. "[This] palace is truly royal; enclosed on one side by the Thames, on the other by a park, which connects it with St. James's, another royal palace," he wrote. Hentzner was especially impressed by the "royal library, well stored with Greek, Latin, Italian and French books" and observed that "All these books are bound in velvet of different colors, though chiefly red, with clasps

THE SPANISH ARMADA

Tensions between England and Spain became especially intense after Elizabeth became queen of England in 1558. Elizabeth's half sister, Mary Tudor, had preceded Elizabeth on the throne and had married Philip II, the King of Spain. Mary and Philip were both ardent Catholics who sought to bring England back into the fold of Catholic Europe. Violent suppression of the resistance of many English Protestants earned the queen the nickname by which she is still known today: "Bloody Mary." When Mary died, Elizabeth succeeded her and showed her new independence in numerous ways, including by refusing Philip's proposal of marriage. In time it became clear that Elizabeth intended to continue the break with Roman Catholicism begun by her father (Henry VIII) and pursued by her half brother (Edward VI)—a break only briefly interrupted by Mary.

Conflict between Spain and England was therefore inevitable. Spain was now the most powerful nation in Europe, and it was attempting to impose its Catholic authority on the Protestant Low Countries, which were directly across the English Channel from England. When the pope excommunicated Elizabeth in February 1570, the queen immediately became, in the eyes of many Catholics, a heretic and a traitor who deserved to be assassinated or overthrown. Various plots against the queen's life and rule were uncovered and severely punished, and increasing numbers of English people began to fear that Spain intended to invade England and reimpose Catholic worship. By the summer of 1588, 130 Spanish ships carrying a large force of troops did appear in English waters with precisely that intention. The English—using small and highly maneuverable ships—inflicted severe damage on the much larger Spanish galleons. Severe weather helped finish the job. The attempted invasion, along with the defeat of the "Spanish Armada," helped solidify the strength of of gold and silver; some have pearls, and precious stones, set in their bindings." He commented on the royal furniture, including silver cabinets, a pearl-encrusted little chest, and even the "queen's bed, ingeniously composed of woods of different colors, with quilts of silk, velvet, gold, silver, and embroidery." He described the royal paintings; various musical instruments, including one on which "two persons may perform at the same time"; and a "piece of clock work" showing "an Ethiop riding upon a Rhinoceros, with four attendants, who all make their obeisance, when it strikes the hour; these are all put into motion by winding up the machine." Hentzner also noted that the park surrounding the palace was full of deer and that in the nearby garden "there is a jet d'eau [jet of water], with a sun dial, which while

Protestantism in England, buttressing Elizabeth's power and reputation as a leader and helping undermine the social, political, and moral position of English Catholics, who were now increasingly viewed as potential traitors.

"I have another weapon in this chamber;
It is a sword of Spain . . ."
— *Othello* (5.2.252–53)

A 1679 illustration of the Spanish Armada. *(Jan Luyken)*

strangers are looking at, a quantity of water, forced by a wheel, which the gardener turns at a distance, through a number of little pipes, plentifully sprinkles those that are standing round." Baron Waldstein also mentioned this fountain at Whitehall, and similar fountains were found at other Elizabethan palaces, suggesting that the queen enjoyed practical jokes.

THE ROYAL PALACE OF HAMPTON COURT

Whitehall was not the only royal palace within easy commuting distance of London. St. James's Palace was another, but the invaluable von Wedel also left us a detailed account of seeing the queen at Hampton Court palace, a huge complex (one of the largest in Europe at the time) that was just a 20-mile boat ride up the Thames from London. Von Wedel reports seeing Elizabeth there in a typically impressive procession on her way to the royal chapel:

> This chapel is well decorated with a beautiful organ, silver gilt, with large and small silver pipes. Before the queen marched her lifeguard, all chosen men, strong and tall, two hundred in number, we were told, though not all of them were present. They bore gilt halberts, red coats faced with black velvet, in front and on the back they wore the queen's arms silver gilt. Then came gentlemen of rank and of the council, two of them bearing a royal sceptre each, a third with the royal sword in a red velvet scabbard, embroidered with gold and set with precious stones and large pearls. Now came the queen, dressed in black [because of the recent deaths of some foreign royals]; on each side of her curly hair she wore a large pearl of the size of a hazelnut.

Wherever Elizabeth went, she was shown respect and was often solicited for help:

> The people standing on both sides fell on their knees, but she showed herself very gracious, and accepted with an humble mien letters of supplication from rich and poor. Her train was carried behind her by a countess, then followed twelve young ladies of noble birth, children of counts or lords, afterwards twenty-four noblemen, called jarseirer [yeomen of the guard] in English, with small gilt hunting spears. There are also one hundred of these, though not all on duty at the same time, for they take it in turns. Both sides of the gallery as far as the queen walked through it to the chapel were lined by the guard

bearing arms. As the day was almost gone there was no sermon, only singing and delivering prayers. Then the queen returned as she had come and went to her rooms, and when on her passing the people fell on their knees, she said in English: 'Thank you with all my heart.' Now eight trumpeters clad in red gave the signal for dinner, and did it very well. Afterwards two drummers and a piper made music according to the English fashion, and we betook ourselves to our lodgings.

Von Wedel's visit to Hampton Court coincided with that of an even more famous visitor, recently home from a far more important voyage:

A ship had arrived having discovered a country or island larger than England and never before visited by Christian people. The master or captain of the ship, named Ral [Sir Walter Raleigh], had brought with him two men of the island whom we asked permission to see. Their faces as well as their whole bodies were very similar to those of the white Moors at home, they wear no shirts, only a piece of fur to cover the pudenda and the skins of wild animals to cover their shoulders. Here they are clad in brown taffeta. Nobody could understand their language, and they had a very childish and wild appearance.

As von Wedel's report reminds us, many unusual people or objects that arrived in England often made their way to the royal court to be personally inspected by the monarch, including "Indians" from the continent of North America.

THE ROYAL PALACE OF GREENWICH

Besides Whitehall and Hampton Court, another favorite royal palace during Shakespeare's era was Greenwich, five miles down the Thames, east of London. Shakespeare mentions this palace only once in his works (*Henry VIII* [1.2.188]), even though he performed there at least twice before Queen Elizabeth. For an impression of the palace, von Wedel is an especially valuable witness, for here as at Hampton Court he actually beheld Elizabeth in person, making her way to and from church services:

During the time she attended public service, a long table was set in the room under the canopy and covered with gold plate. When the queen left the church, forty dishes, small and large, all silver gilt, were put on the table, and she sat down quite alone by herself. She never during the whole year dines publicly, except on festival days, when strangers may see her dine. At the end of the room close to the door there is a table set for five countesses to take dinner after the queen's dinner is finished. The queen is served at dinner by a very young gentleman in black, who carves; the drink is handed to her by one in green, almost of the same age, who has to kneel while she drinks. Afterwards he rises again and takes the cup from her. To the right side of the table stand the gentlemen of high rank. . . . They all had white sticks in their hands and were fine old gentlemen. It is the queen's habit to call one of them to her and to converse with him. When she does so, he has to kneel until she orders him to rise. When they leave the queen, they have to bow down deeply, and when they have reached the middle of the room they must bow down a second time.

When dinner was served, the servants had to

march before the nobles and gentlemen, bearing the dishes, which this time were only twenty-four. On entering the room with the dishes, they bow down three times, as well as on spreading the table-cloth and setting the plates, even though the queen should not be present. Four sceptre bearers march before the queen when she goes to dinner. As long as dinner lasts, ladies and gentlemen stand on both sides of the room near those who have the charge of the plate, which is truly of imperial character, but not too near to the royal table. The music during the dinner was very good. When the first dishes were removed and replaced by others, the queen did not remain much longer, but rose from the table. Then the five countesses aforesaid rose from their table, made two very low obeisances to the queen and then stood aside, upon which the queen rose, went to the other side of her table, leaning with her back against it, when two bishops placed themselves before her to say grace.

Then the queen was presented with

a very large covered basin of silver-gilt like a dish, whilst two of the old gentlemen carried the bowl. On approaching the queen, all five knelt down, took the cover from the basin, and whilst two held the lower part of it, the third with the cover poured the water out for the queen. Before washing, the queen handed a ring to one of the chamberlains mentioned, and afterwards took it again from him. Then she took the son of a count by his mantle and stepped with him to a bow window, where he knelt before her and held a long conversation with her. When he had left her, she took a cushion and sat down on the floor, called another young gentleman, who also knelt down on his knees and spoke with her, after him she called a countess, who knelt down to her in the same manner as the gentlemen.

At this point,

dancing began and the ladies and gentlemen took each other by the hands as in Germany. The gentlemen had their hats and caps on, though at other times nobody, high or low, is permitted to keep his hat on his head in the Queen's chamber, whether she be present or not. They danced one behind the other as in Germany, and most of the ladies and gentlemen had gloves on. In the beginning the dance appeared to be in the German fashion, but afterwards it differed from it; the partners advanced a few paces, stepped back again, separated, changed their places, but in the right moment everybody found his partner again. During the dance they often bowed to each other and the gentlemen took their hats off to the ladies, among whom were indeed some very beautiful persons sumptuously dressed. This dance or dances were performed only by the highest in rank, who had passed youth, but afterwards the young people took off their swords and mantles, and in hoses and jackets invited the ladies to the galliard with them.

Elizabeth loved to dance and also loved to view dancing, and von Wedel reports that

The queen addressed those who had danced well. When this was over the queen gave a sign to her suite and went to her room. At this moment I left also, took a boat and rowed the five miles back again to London. The queen, as long as the dance lasted, had ordered old and young persons to come and converse with her, who, as I have mentioned, were all obliged to kneel on their knees before her. She talked to them in a very friendly manner, making jokes, and to a captain named *Ral* [Sir Walter Raleigh] she pointed with her finger in his face, saying he had some uncleanness there, which she even intended to wipe off with her handkerchief. He, however, prevented her and took it away himself. It was said that she loved this gentleman now in preference to all others; and that may be well believed, for two years ago he was scarcely able to keep a single servant, and now she has bestowed so much upon him, that he is able to keep five hundred servants.

COURTIERS' LIVES (AND DEATHS): SIR WALTER RALEIGH, WILLIAM PARR, AND THE EARL OF ARUNDEL

Von Wedel provides one of the most vivid and comprehensive (if little known) of all surviving accounts of what life was like, and how life was lived, at the royal court in Shakespeare's age. His closing reference to Raleigh is especially interesting, because that reference suggests how much any courtier depended, for good or ill, on the personal favor of courtly patrons, especially if one's patron happened to be the monarch. As von Wedel's remarks suggest, Sir Walter Raleigh enjoyed one of the most spectacular rises of any courtier during Elizabeth's reign, but he also experienced a number of devastating falls during his life at court, both under Elizabeth and under her successor, King James I. He spent much of his life during James's reign confined in the Tower of London. Briefly released, he was executed in 1618. Few lives illustrate better than Raleigh's how uncertain and unpredictable anyone's standing at court could be—how fast one could rise and how far one could fall.

Immediately after mentioning Raleigh, von Wedel recounts an incident showing that even the monarch's position was far from safe. The episode that von Wedel recounts reminds one of Brutus's famous words, in Shakespeare's *Julius Caesar*, that "conspiracy" is often hidden in "smiles and affability" (2.1.82):

> In the year 1585, March 2, the queen ordered one of her doctors of law to be executed for having sought after her life, which took place in the following manner. The said doctor had made his studies in Italy, had visited Rome, and sought intercourse with the cardinals. After having made their acquaintance, he had offered to kill the queen, if this would be agreeable to the Pope, because the Queen of England was not of Popish religion. This pleased the Pope, who, if the doctor succeeded in his scheme, promised him Heaven. Thereupon the doctor, whose name was William Perre [Parr], returned to England,

Portrait of Sir Walter Raleigh, 1588. *(artist unknown)*

and, being a learned scholar, found access to the queen, who liked him very much.

Ironically, it was thanks to the queen that Parr was taken into favor and his life was spared for the commission of an earlier crime, because

> once by the committing of some crime he had forfeited his life, [but] she released him, took him to the court, and bestowed upon him [a substantial] annuity . . . , which shows that she meant well by him.

He, however, was all the time seeking an opportunity to take her life. At last he found a person whom he made a partner of the plot, charging him to give his assistance in effecting his plan. The day having been fixed, the doctor entered the queen's chamber, where she was by herself, with a knife hidden in his sleeve, intending to stab her. The queen, however, when she observed him, asked, 'Doctor, do you know what dream I had this night?' On his replying 'No,' she remarked, 'I dreamed I had a vein opened and lost much blood.' The doctor on hearing this got frightened, thinking she had discovered the plot, and fainted, upon which the queen, who was much attached to him, called for medical help. For she was of opinion that the dream had frightened him so much because he loved her, and for this she esteemed him the more.

Parr, however, continued to plot against the queen, but when his partner eventually confessed the conspiracy, Parr confessed as well. He was

imprisoned for a few days and then transported on a slide through the whole town from the Tower to Westminster, where, after being hung on the gallows, he was cut down again and quartered [that is, cut into four parts]. Some time before eighteen individuals, and among these two women and two boys, were all together hung on the gallows in this way. They were put on a cart and when the cart was driven on they were left hanging; but they did not remain there very long. Their friends came, pulled them by the legs, and struck them on the chest, to end their lives the sooner, and when life was gone, they cut them off and buried them.

Parr's mutilated corpse suffered a different fate than the corpses of these common criminals:

The Doctor's head was fixed on the gate of London Bridge, where about thirty heads of noblemen and gentlemen were fixed who had sought to take the life of the queen. The queen, when she heard this about the doctor, went into the garden, wept aloud, and said she would like to know why so many persons sought her life. She tore open her garment, exposing her breasts, exclaiming that she had no weapon to defend herself, but was only a weak female. She would trust in God Almighty, that He would have mercy upon her.

Even for the monarch the court could be a place of genuine insecurity and danger. ("Uneasy lies the head that wears a crown," remarks King Henry in *2 Henry IV* [3.1.31].) The monarch was surrounded by numerous people, many of them armed, who had sworn allegiance to the ruler but who might be convinced that some higher allegiance took precedence. Shakespeare's play *Julius Caesar* memorably depicts the assassination of one very powerful ruler; *Macbeth* depicts the murder of another. Because of the conflict between Catholics and Protestants during this period, Elizabeth's life was particularly vulnerable. Indeed, not long after recounting the conspiracy involving Doctor Parr, von Wedel recounts yet another one involving the Earl of Arundel, who had attempted to leave England without the queen's permission, allegedly to plot against her abroad. He spent the rest of his life in the Tower, where he died of dysentery after 10 years. Elizabeth knew, as well as Henry V does in Shakespeare's play, that sometimes those who professed the most loyalty to a monarch could be trusted the least. Thus the Earl of Cambridge, even as he plots against Henry, tells him, "Never was monarch better fear'd and lov'd / Than is your Majesty. There's not, I think, a subject / That sits in heart-grief and uneasiness / Under the sweet shade of your government" (2.2.25–28). Shortly after he utters these words, his conspiracy against the king is exposed and punished with death.

A COURTIER'S LIFE: SIR ROBERT CARY

However insecure life might seem to the monarch, it was even less secure for any royal courtier, of whatever rank. A courtier's fate and fortune depended on the good opinion of the monarch—if the courtier was even prominent enough to be known by the monarch at all—and on the good opinions of numerous others, including many who might be rivals and competitors. Robert Cary left one of the best surviving accounts of how it felt to live as a courtier under Queen Elizabeth and King James. Cary eventually rose to the status of Earl of Monmouth, but only after decades of frustration and disappointment. Cary's rise began when he was a young man and happened to visit Scotland as part of an English delegation. There, he notes, "it pleased the King [King James VI] at that time to take such a liking to me, as he wrote earnestly to the Queen at [the delegation's] return to give me leave to come back to him again, to attend on him at his court, assuring her Majesty I should not repent my attendance." Thus, a chance encounter with the King of Scotland had brought Cary to a certain prominence, both in

KING JAMES VI & I

James Stuart, the sixth king of Scotland named James and the first king of England so named, was a controversial figure in his own day and has also been a figure of controversy among historians. As successor to Elizabeth I, one of the most famous and popular monarchs in English history, James almost inevitably suffered by comparison with his charismatic predecessor. He lacked the instinctive popular touch that made Elizabeth such an effective ruler, but the fact that he was from Scotland, and that he brought with him many Scottish courtiers, also bothered some of his English subjects at the time and seems to have been a source of condescension among subsequent English commentators and historians. James's intention to unite his two kingdoms into a realm known as "Great Britain" was also resisted by many people in England, who thought that their country had little to gain (especially financially) from such a union.

James was a highly intellectual king who produced many books on many subjects (including kingship, tobacco, and witchcraft), but he was also perceived by some of his new subjects as somewhat uncouth and too busy with pleasurable pastimes, especially hunting. His attraction to handsome young men, who often became powerful favorites, also aroused suspicion. Yet the king was married and had fathered several children, three of whom survived.

King James I of England, ca. 1621. (Daniel Mytens)

James ruled England during a time of immense religious tension. He had to deal not only with disgruntled Catholics but also disgruntled Puritans, and he was rarely able to keep anyone entirely happy about religious matters. His reign was also a time of political dissension, especially among those who were troubled by the king's emphasis on royal power. James, nevertheless, is increasingly seen as a relatively successful king who kept England out of war and who certainly ruled with more skill, wisdom, and tact than the son who succeeded him as Charles I.

"From Scotland am I stol'n, even of pure love,
To greet mine own land with my wishful sight."
— *3 Henry VI* (3.1.13–14)

Edinburgh and London. The queen at first agreed to let Cary return to James, but then she suddenly changed her mind— an example of how fickle a monarch's opinion could be and of how much depended on such unpredictable alterations of mood or opinion.

In 1587 Cary was sent again as an ambassador to King James, a role that would prove highly important to him later in life. In 1588, back in England, he fought the invading Spanish Armada. In 1589 he solidified his financial position at court but then became involved in 1591 in one of the queen's frequent quarrels with her new favorite, the Earl of Essex, who had disobeyed her command to return to London immediately from the Continent, where he was involved in a military expedition. Before the queen's command had reached him, Essex had won an important victory and had dispatched Cary to court

Portrait of Robert Devereux, second Earl of Essex, who led a failed rebellion against Queen Elizabeth I. *(Marcus Gheeraerts the Younger)*

to explain his failure to obey her orders. "I spake with most of the Council before the Queen was stirring, who assured me that there was no removing of her Majesty from her resolution, and advised me to take heed that I gave her no cause to be offended with me, by persuading her for his stay," Cary reports. When Cary finally met with Elizabeth, she was indeed furious with Essex. Cary wisely, waited before speaking, but then warned the queen that if she recalled Essex now, the earl would be so ashamed that he would abandon the court and "retire to some cell in the country, and . . . live there, as a man never desirous to look a good man in the face again." Cary claimed to have told the queen, "And in good faith, Madam, to deal truly with your Majesty, I think you will not have him a long-lived man after his return." Cary warned the queen that she would break Essex's heart: "Then your majesty will have sufficient satisfaction for the offence he hath committed against you."

Not surprisingly, the queen "seemed to be something offended at my discourse, and bade me go to dinner." Shortly thereafter, Cary received a letter, handwritten by the queen, that instructed Cary to tell Essex that if anything in the letter pleased him, he should thank Cary for that. Thus Cary's eloquence had won the day— for him and for Essex. When Essex returned to court, he had "expected nothing but her Majesty's heavy displeasure [but]he found it clean contrary, for she used him with that grace and favor, that he stayed a week with her, passing the time in jollity and feasting; and then with tears in her eyes, she showed her affection to him, and for the repair of his honor gave him leave to return to his charge again." Everyone involved knew, though, how easily things might have turned out differently: The queen might well have remained angry, Essex could have lost his status and his reputation, and Cary might have fallen along with his patron if his patron had taken a fall. The court could be a slippery slope indeed.

Essex was grateful to Cary for the latter's intervention on his behalf; he embraced Cary and promised never to forget Cary's help. Even the queen looked favorably on Cary, at least for a while: At one point she relieved his debts using money from the public treasury, but it was not long afterward that Cary, only 31, felt he had "passed [his] best time in court, and got little" and so "betook [himself] to the country," where he "lived with great content." (Thus Belarius in *Cymbeline* contrasts the simplicity of life in the countryside with the vanity of service at court: "O, this life / Is nobler than attending for a check; / Richer than doing nothing for a bauble; / Prouder than rustling in unpaid-for silk" [3.3.21–24].) Yet the incident that seems to have come closest to ruining Cary's standing with the queen and with her court was his decision to marry, in the countryside, without the queen's approval. As Cary describes the events, "I married a gentlewoman more for her worth than her wealth . . . [nor] did she marry me for any great wealth . . . [and] I was near a thousand pounds in debt. The queen, he reports, "was mightily offended with me for marrying," as were most of his "best friends, only my father was no ways displeased at it, which gave me great content." Even Cary's own brother plotted against him, at least by Cary's account, in a separate legal matter, for the brother "assured himself I durst not come near the court, having so lately offended the Queen, and the most of my friends by my marriage." But Cary traveled to London and prevailed against his brother. With the queen still angry with him, Cary hit upon an idea that would occur only to an Elizabethan courtier: He participated, in disguise, in the annual Accession Day tilt, presenting himself as a forsaken but devoted knight. This pleased the queen, and so he made himself "known in court, and for the time I stayed there I was daily conversant with my own companions and friends."

Cary did not stay at court for long, however, because King James of Scotland sent word that he had an urgent message for the queen and he would entrust that message only to a member of Cary's family. Told of this, the queen said to Cary's father,

> "I hear your fine son that has lately married so worthily, is
> hereabouts; send him if you will to know the King's pleasure." My
> father answered, he knew I would be glad to obey her commands. "No
> (said she) do you bid him go, for I have nothing to do with him." My
> father came and told me what had passed between them. I thought
> it hard to be sent, and not to see her, but my father told me plainly,
> that she would neither speak with me nor see me. "Sir," said I, "if she
> be on such hard terms with me, I had need be wary what I do. If I go
> to the King without her license, it were in her power to hang me at
> my return, and for anything I see, it were ill [that is, unwise] trusting
> her." My father merrily went to the Queen, and told her what I said.
> She answered, "If the gentleman be so untrustful, let the Secretary
> make a safe conduct to go and come, and I will sign it."

Cary then departed for Scotland, received a signed letter from James to Elizabeth explaining James's important business as Cary did not want the responsibility of reporting the news orally, and then returned quickly to England.

> I made all the haste I could to court, which was then at Hampton
> Court. I arrived there on St. Stephen's day in the afternoon. Dirty as
> I was, I came into the presence, where I found the lords and ladies
> dancing. The Queen was not there. My father went to the Queen,
> to let her know that I was returned. She willed him to take my
> message or letters, and bring them to her. He came for them, but I
> desired him to excuse me; for that which I had to say either by word
> or by writing, I must deliver myself. I could neither trust him, nor
> much less any other therewith. He acquainted her Majesty with my
> resolution. With much ado I was called for in; and I was left alone
> with her. Our first encounter was stormy and terrible, which I passed
> over with silence.

Many people would have been at a real loss for words at this point, but Cary reports what happened next:

> After she had spoken her pleasure of me and my wife, I told her, that "She herself was the fault of my marriage, and that if she had but graced me with the least of her favors, I had never left her nor her court; and seeing she was the chief cause of my misfortune, I would never off my knees till I had kissed her hand, and obtained my pardon."

The logic of that final sentence might puzzle many people today (why should Cary seek the queen's pardon if she had caused his misfortune?), but to Elizabeth it made perfect sense:

> She was not displeased with my excuse, and before we parted we grew good friends. Then I delivered my message and my papers, which she took very well, and at last gave me thanks for the pains I had taken. So having her princely word that she had pardoned and forgotten all faults, I kissed her hand, and came forth to the presence, and was in the court, as I was ever before.
>
> This God did for me to bring me in favor with my sovereign; for if this occasion had been slipped, it may be I should never, never have seen her face more.

This incident reveals the typical existence of a Renaissance courtier. Cary had left the court because he felt he was not prospering there; he decided to marry for love rather than wealth; his marriage offended the queen and therefore exposed him to the disapproval of many others and the stratagems of his own brother; by mere chance he was able to do the queen a service that only he could perform; and, because he was willing to be outspoken and deeply humble, he was restored to the queen's favor and thus to favor in the court. His restoration, of course, was never entirely secure, but for the time being Robert Cary could hold his head high again. As a character exclaims in Shakespeare's *Henry VIII*, "O, how wretched / Is that poor man that hangs on princes' favors!" (3.2.366–67).

THE COURT IN PROGRESS AND PROCESSION

The royal court was never really settled in one place. The monarch, and therefore the court, was often moving from one palace to another or from one smaller royal residence to the next. The court also moved across the countryside, from one town or village to another. Elizabeth, in particular, saw these royal "progresses" as especially important ways of displaying herself and her power to her people and of maintaining contact with the most and least powerful subjects in her land. Whenever the monarch left London on one of these "progresses," large numbers of courtiers, servants, soldiers, horses, and carts went along. When James became king, he quickly reduced the number of carts that had been used for progresses during Elizabeth's reign from 600 to 220, but he also faced a variety of more serious complaints. The most important of these involved "purveyance" and "purveyors." These words refer to the right of court officials, during the progresses, to buy up all kinds of local products and services (including additional carts) at favorable rates, even if potential local purchasers suffered as a result. Residents in the countryside, villages, and towns often looked forward to a visit by a monarch, but they dreaded some aspects of such visits. The visits involved massive expenses and significant disruptions of normal routines, and much of the cost was borne by the local communities, especially any wealthy person "lucky" enough to host the royal party. (Surely some of these subjects must have agreed with the character in *1 Henry VI* who repeats the proverb that "unbidden guests / Are often welcomest when they are gone" [2.2.55–56].)

Among the most interesting accounts of royal progresses involve the trip Elizabeth undertook in the late summer of 1591. Progresses often occurred during the hotter months of the year so courtiers could escape the heat of London, as well as accompanying hot-weather diseases. By Saturday, August 15, 1591, for instance, the queen had come "with a great train to the Right Honorable the Lord Mountague's . . . about eight of the clock at night; where, upon sight of her Majesty, loud music sounded, which at her entrance on the bridge suddenly ceased. Then was a speech delivered by a personage in armor, standing between two porters, carved out of wood, he resembling the third; holding his club in one hand, and a key of gold in the other." The queen listened to the porter's unusually brief speech and then "her Highness took the key, and said, she would swear for him, there was none more faithful: then being alighted, she embraced the Lady Montecute [sic], and the Lady Dortnir her daughter. The Mistress of the house (as it were weeping in her bosom) said, "O happy time, O joyful day!" Later that evening, the queen "took her rest; and so in like manner the next day, which was Sunday, being most Royally feasted. The proportion of breakfast was three oxen, and one hundred and forty geese," which suggests a sizeable celebration. The account then continues:

> On Monday, at eight of the clock in the morning, her Highness took horse, with all her train, and rode into the park: where was a delicate bower prepared, under which were her Highness's musicians placed, and a cross-bow by a Nymph, with a sweet song, delivered to her hands, to shoot at the deer, about some thirty in number, put into a paddock [enclosed field], of which number she killed three or four, and the Countess of Kildare one.
>
> Then rode her Grace to Cowdry to dinner, and about six of the clock in the evening, from a turret, saw sixteen bucks . . . pulled down with greyhounds, in a laund [pasture].
>
> On Tuesday her Majesty went to dinner to the Priory, where my Lord himself kept house; and there was she and her Lords most bountifully feasted.
>
> After dinner she came to view my Lord's walks, where she was met by a Pilgrim, clad in a coat of russet velvet, fashioned to his calling; his hat being of the same, with scallop-shells of cloth of silver . . . .

This "pilgrim," planted at the scene to fulfill a specific role, then delivered to the queen the usual witty and complimentary speech, after which "did the Pilgrim conduct her Highness to an Oak not far off, whereon her Majesty's arms, and all the arms of the Noblemen and Gentlemen of that Shire were hanged in escutcheons most beautiful." Next appeared a person dressed up as a "wild man," who explained the significance of the tree in lengthy detail. At the conclusion of his speech, "upon the winding of a cornet, was a most excellent cry of hounds, and three bucks killed by the buck hounds, and so went all back to Cowdry to supper." Meanwhile, "on Wednesday the Lords and Ladies dined in the walks, feasted most sumptuously at a table four and twenty yards long. In the beginning, her Majesty coming to take the pleasure of the walks, was delighted with most delicate music, and brought to a goodly fish-pond, where was an Angler [fisherman]." The angler pretended, at first, to take "no notice of her Majesty," but then he delivered a speech mixing comedy with real social satire, thus fulfilling part of the deeper purpose of these entertainments, which were supposed to mix serious counsel with clever compliments. Apparently Elizabeth listened respectfully; then, after eating, she went hunting once more.

The 1588 "Armada" portrait of Queen Elizabeth I. *(George Gower)*

On Thursday the queen "dined in the privy walks in the garden, and the Lords and Ladies at a table of forty-eight yards long. In the evening the country people presented themselves to her Majesty in a pleasant dance, with taber and pipe; and the Lord Montague and his Lady among them, to the great pleasure of all the beholders, and gentle applause of her Majesty." On Friday the queen departed for Chichester (having stayed nearly a week at Cowdry), but not before creating six new knights, including the son and son-in-law of her host. Thus the visit ended: Elizabeth and her court had enjoyed themselves at the expense of a prominent local nobleman; the nobleman had displayed his estate, generosity, and worthiness to the queen and the court; and the queen had been on display before—and had mingled with—prominent local subjects and even some of the humbler "country people." Massive amounts of food had been consumed; much hunting and killing of deer had been accomplished (a favorite sport of monarchs and one often mentioned by Shakespeare); and someone had even gone to the trouble of writing speeches for the event and putting on small bits of dramatic entertainment. The queen had enjoyed herself, and her host had been rewarded by the prestige of a royal visit.

In nearly all these respects, the queen's visit to Cowdry was a typical example of a royal progress during Shakespeare's era. For the host, much depended on the success of these events. This much is clear from the careful instructions given by the Earl of Hertford to his own servants about a month after the queen visited Cowdry. At this point, in late September, she was still making her progress and was about to arrive at the earl's estate. That morning, "about nine of the clock, when every other needful place or point of service was established and set in order for so great an entertainment," the earl "called for, and drew all his servants into the chief thicket of the park: where in few words he put them in mind what quietness, and what diligence, or other duty, they were to use at that present: that their service might first work her Majesty's content, and thereby his honor; and lastly, their own credit; with the increase of his love and favor towards them." The earl knew that everyone had to cooperate to please the queen. If the queen was pleased, the earl would be pleased, and if the earl was pleased, his servants could expect an "increase of his love and favor towards them."

Fortunately for the earl, the queen was indeed pleased. At one point during her visit, for instance, the "spectacle and music so delighted her Majesty, that she commanded to hear it sung and to be danced three times over, and called for diverse Lords and Ladies to behold it: and then dismissed the Actors with thanks, and with a gracious largesse, which of her exceeding goodness she bestowed upon them." At the conclusion of the visit, she was "so highly pleased" with the final show and with "the rest, that she openly said to the Earl of Hertford, that the beginning, process, and end of this his entertainment, was so honorable, she would not forget the same." Hertford and his servants had thus accomplished their fundamental goal of pleasing the queen, and no doubt they were highly pleased as a result. Progresses such as the ones just described help to demonstrate vividly that the court, in a real sense, existed wherever the monarch happened to be. Contact and interaction with the monarch essentially defined the court, and this became especially obvious 12 years later, when Queen Elizabeth lay on her deathbed.

THE QUEEN IS DEAD; LONG LIVE THE KING

One of the most famous accounts of the last days of Queen Elizabeth, and also of the transfer of power to King James VI of Scotland, was left by Robert Cary. Having kept away from the court for several years, Cary happened to visit not long before Elizabeth's death. "When I came to court," he writes, "I found the Queen ill disposed, and she kept her inner lodging; yet she, hearing of my arrival, sent for me." When Cary said that he was happy to see her in safety and good health, "She took me by the hand, and wrung it hard, and said 'No, Robin, I am not well,' and then discoursed with me of her indisposition, and that her heart had been sad and heavy for ten or twelve days, and in her discourse she fetched not so few as forty or fifty great sighs." As Cary and the other courtiers could see that the queen was in rapid decline, Cary inevitably considered what her death would mean for his fortunes: "I could not but think in what a wretched estate I should be left [if she died], most of my livelihood depending on her life." He assured himself that "it was neither unjust nor unhonest for me to do for myself, if God at that time should call her to his mercy." He thus wrote to King James in Scotland, with whom he had long had friendly contact, and "desired him not to stir from Edinburgh; if of that sickness she should die, I would be the first man that should bring him news of it."

The queen did die after indicating that she wanted James of Scotland to be her successor. At this point, Cary sought to leave the palace and head directly to Edinburgh, but he was led "to the privy chamber, where all the Council was assembled; there I was caught hold of, and assured I should not go to Scotland, till their pleasures were farther known." At this point the court, technically, was now in Edinburgh with the new king, who did not even know at this point that he was the new king. The members of the Privy Council apparently were thinking of sending their own messenger to inform James of his succession, but Cary, with the help of a brother who was a court official, managed to slip free of the palace. Even then he did not immediately leave for Scotland but waited to hear what the Privy Council wanted him to do. One member of the council sent word to Cary that if he returned to the palace, as some council members wanted him to do, he would be detained. So he departed immediately for Scotland, riding as fast as he could and suffering a serious fall along the way.

Arriving in Edinburgh, Cary was graciously received by King James, who instructed his personal physician to attend to Cary's injuries. James promised Cary that he would be "as good a master to you" as Queen Elizabeth had been and also promised to requite Cary's "service with honor and reward." Cary soon asked to be made a gentleman of the king's bedchamber—a strategically important position that would give him close and

THE GUNPOWDER PLOT

Although many Catholics in England had hoped that their religion would be better tolerated after King James VI of Scotland became King James I of England in 1603, they were quickly disappointed. Persecution of Catholics slackened at first but soon resumed, and any hope that foreign Catholic powers might intervene on behalf of their English co-religionists eventually evaporated. By the winter of 1604, a small group of radical Catholics centered on Robert Catesby had devised a plan to eliminate King James and most of the Protestant ruling class at once. Catesby and his fellow conspirators planned to hide many barrels of gunpowder directly beneath the parliamentary House of Lords and literally blow the government to pieces when the king, commons, and lords next assembled for the opening of Parliament. James's young daughter, Princess Elizabeth, would not be present for the event, so she would be seized and used as a pliable new monarch.

This complicated plan came close to succeeding. Even though the government was warned in a mysterious letter that something was afoot, and even though the king suspected that gunpowder might be involved, the hidden powder was not immediately discovered by those searching for it. It was eventually found, and one of the conspirators—Guy Fawkes—was apprehended at the scene. He confessed under torture, and the other conspirators were quickly tracked down and captured after a bloody fight. The Gunpowder Plot became legendary in English history and made Catholics an even more despised and distrusted minority than they already were. King James did not blame the entire Catholic population for the conspiracy, but not all of his subjects were as almost constant contact with the monarch. James agreed, and so Cary's fortunes in the new reign looked quite promising. Cary would automatically lose a lucrative position he had held under Elizabeth. Nevertheless, he writes that "Most of the great ones in court envied my happiness when they heard I was sworn of the King's bedchamber," even though "in Scotland I had no acquaintance. I only relied on God and the King. The one never left me, the other shortly after his coming to London deceived my expectation, and adhered to those that sought my ruin."

This last sentence is a reminder that the life of a courtier in Shakespeare's time was never secure, even when it began as promisingly as Cary's did under the reign of King James. In fact, the very prominence that a person such as Cary seemed to enjoy would have made him the inevitable target of others' envy and maneuverings, especially if they detected any vulnerability

reasonable as he. The date associated with the plot's discovery—November 5, 1605—is still commemorated in England today as a time of celebration and thanksgiving.

"These violent delights have violent ends
And in their triumph die, like fire and powder,
Which as they kiss consume."
— *Romeo and Juliet* (2.6.9–11)

Detail from a contemporary engraving of the Gunpowder Plot conspirators.

in his position. Thus, James no sooner arrived in London than Cary was dismissed, at least temporarily, from the bedchamber and given a lesser position: "I could not help it. Those that ruled the helm had so resolved it; and I was forced to that I could not help. All the comfort that I had was the King's assurance that I should shortly be admitted to his bedchamber again." Cary was warned, moreover, not to appear displeased. One of his enemies gave him the best advice: "He told me he knew the King better than I did, and assured me that if the King did perceive in me a discontented mind, I should never have his love nor favor again. I had a sad heart, yet before the King I showed myself merry and jovial." The court was a place of personal drama: One had to play a part or several parts; one had to present the right face to the right people; and one often had to disguise one's true feelings before anyone powerful, especially if sincerity might be poorly received.

Cary never was admitted to the bedchamber, despite the king's promise. It was through his wife's involvement with Prince Charles, the king's unhealthy youngest son, that Cary's fortunes began to improve. The prince (also known as "the duke") needed someone to oversee his care. Cary reports that "There were many great ladies [who were] suitors for the keeping of the Duke; but when they did see how weak a child he was, and not likely to live, their hearts were down, and none of them were desirous to take charge of him." The queen chose Cary's wife to care for her son. "Those who wished me no good," Cary reports, "were glad of it, thinking that if the Duke should die in our charge (his weakness being such as gave them great cause to suspect it) then it would not be thought fit that we should remain in court after." The duke, however, thrived under the guardianship of Cary's wife, and the Lady Cary therefore rose in the estimation of the king and queen. Thanks to the intervention of Cary's wife, Cary later received a highly profitable favor from the king. To add to their good fortune, the Carys' daughter became intimate with "the King's daughter and served her, and had the happiness to be allowed to wait on her in the privy lodgings. My wife and self, by waiting still in the privy lodgings of the Duke, got better esteem of the King and Queen."

Merely by being at court, Cary was one of the most powerful people in the entire kingdom, but his power and prestige never felt secure to him. Cary knew they could be lost at any time and that the humiliation of losing power was almost worse than never having enjoyed it in the first place. In the long run, Cary prospered: The young duke for whom his wife had once cared eventually became king after the duke's older brother unexpectedly died, and Cary was rewarded for his family's good service to (and close connections with) the new monarch. The last words of Cary's main narrative are as follows: "I was created Earl of Monmouth." But that happy outcome could never have been predicted. At any moment, for any reason, the life of a courtier such as Robert Cary could either suffer a dramatic fall or enjoy a welcome season of prosperity. And what was true for Cary was often true for people more powerful than he, most especially the king or queen.

Sources and Further Reading

Cary, Sir Robert. *Memoirs of Robert Cary, Earl of Monmouth.* Ed. G. H. Powell. London: Alexander Moring, 1905. Print.

Loades, David. *The Tudor Court.* Revised ed. Bangor, Wales: Headstart History, 1992. Print.

Von Wedel, Leopold. "Journey Through England and Scotland in the Years 1584 and 1585." Trans. G. von Billow. *Transactions of the Royal Historical Society* n.s. 9 (1895) 228-70. Print.

BIBLIOGRAPHY

Bridenbaugh, Carl. *Vexed and Troubled Englishmen 1590–1642*. New York: Oxford University Press, 1968. Print.

Burton, Elizabeth. *The Elizabethans at Home*. London: Secker & Warburg, 1958. Print.

Emerson, Kathy Lynn. *The Writer's Guide to Everyday Life in Renaissance England from 1485–1649*. Cincinnati, OH: Writer's Digest Books, 1996. Print.

Fritze, Ronald H. *Historical Dictionary of Tudor England, 1485–1603*. New York: Greenwood, 1991. Print.

Harrison, William. *The Description of England*. Ed. Georges Edelen. Ithaca, NY: Cornell University Press, 1968. Print.

Hentzner, Paul. *Paul Hentzner's Travels in England During the Reign of Queen Elizabeth*. Trans. Horace, Late Earl of Oxford. London: Edward Jeffrey, 1797. Modernized by S. Rhoads. Print. Available online. URL: http://www.elfinspell.com/HentznerModern.html.

Kinney, Arthur F. and David W. Swain, eds. *Tudor England: An Encyclopedia*. New York: Garland, 2001. Print.

Pinciss, Gerald M. and Roger Lockyer, eds. *Shakespeare's World: Background Readings in the English Renaissance*. New York: Continuum, 1989. Print.

Pritchard, R. E., ed. *Shakespeare's England: Life in Elizabethan and Jacobean Times*. Phoenix Mill, Gloucestershire: Sutton, 1999. Print.

Scott, A. F. *Every One a Witness: The Stuart Age*. New York: Thomas Y. Crowell, 1975. Print.

———. *Every One a Witness: The Tudor Age*. New York: Thomas Y. Crowell, 1975. Print.

Shakespeare, William. *The Riverside Shakespeare*. 2nd ed. Boston: Houghton Mifflin, 1997. Print.

Sharpe, J. A. *Early Modern England: A Social History 1550–1760*. 2nd ed. New York: Oxford University Press, 1997. Print.

Singman, Jeffrey. *Daily Life in Elizabethan England*. Westport, CT: Greenwood, 1995.

[Waldstein, Baron.] Valdstejna, Zdenek Brtnický z, baron. *The Diary of Baron Waldstein, A Traveller in Elizabethan England*. Translated and annotated by G. W. Groos. London: Thames and Hudson, 1981. Print.

Wilson, John Dover. *Life in Shakespeare's England*. 1911. London: Penguin, 1944.

INDEX

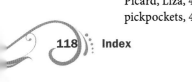